MW00897776

There comes a time when you read a
your being; *ELEVATED* is such a book! Kenneth Hill takes the most
intimate relationship, his walk with Father God, and relates it in terms
of his life, family, work, and community. We see ourselves in these pages.
We hear ourselves in the dialogue recounted. We measure ourselves as
we watch Kenneth listen to God in spite of what is popular, right, or
clear. We acknowledge that everything that we endure is indeed for our
good, for our benefit, and for our development. If you are intentional
in moving forward with your life, career, marriage, or relationship with
God...PLEASE READ THIS BOOK!

Dr. John L. Mason, Educator, Trainer,
Student Ambassador, and Author of *Purifire:
Using the Storms of Life to Ignite Your Life's Purpose*

ELEVATED tells the life journey of Kenneth Hill and the way he experienced God at work in his heart. If your journey does not develop scar
tissue, you are not ready for God's real work for you to fulfill. Kenneth
shares the REAL story of his spiritual journey and the impact one can
make when he is submitted to God's will. *ELEVATED* is a must-read
of anyone who wants to be a servant leader in this Kairos moment.

Dr. John Posey - Area Director
CBMC Metro Atlanta

In *ELEVATED*, Kenneth Hill takes us on a personal journey littered
with transparent monumental moments. Each moment from his life
offers a tremendous deal of insight into the developmental process of
every son and daughter of God. He masterfully unlocks the door of
despair brought on by disappointment and awakens us to what it truly
means to be a partaker of God's divine nature. *ELEVATED* is a must
read for anyone that has found themselves trapped in the web of fear and

needs the steady hand of love to lift you out of your dire situation. Get ready to grow; Get ready to be changed; Get ready to be *ELEVATED*!

Jerome Dial - Senior Pastor,
Founder Vision Faith Church,
The REACH International

When Kenneth Hill calls the answer is "YES!" That's how much I respect his integrity and walk with Christ. Kenneth's life story is an illustration of his love for the Lord and people. You will be blessed and inspired by his new book – *ELEVATED*. Enjoy!

Boyd Bailey – President National Christian
Foundation (Atlanta, Georgia)

In his book *ELEVATED*, Kenneth Hill tells a remarkable and compelling story of one man's journey to a deeper and more meaningful relationship with Jesus Christ. This journey led him to a unique and exciting life that has impacted and transformed the lives of thousands. I believe that you will find great encouragement as you read, but more than that, I know you will find the truth of how the grace, mercy, forgiveness, and love of Jesus can change our world. Thank you, Kenny, for sharing this powerful story.

Dr. George Dillard - Sr. Pastor
Peachtree City Christian Church

Kenneth Hill has penned an authentic and most inspiring life journey with bold sincerity and relevance about the challenging personal, business, social, and life issues he faced in a 30-year career with The Home Depot in his book, *ELEVATED*. You will be invited into these challenges as you identify with his internal struggles and searches for direction regarding the ultimate purpose in life. Kenny skillfully shows you through many Biblical Scriptures how God is always mindful and at work in your life to heal, overcome, reward, and provide His victory through Jesus Christ. The kind of Co-Laboring with God discussed in *ELEVATED* will call you to a higher call of embracing the principles of God's Kingdom and a lifestyle as taught and demonstrated by Jesus Christ. Enjoy what can happen when you too learn how-to walk-in faith, hope, and love!

W. J. Webb, Theological Ethicist

ELEVATED

ELEVATED

My Journey to Co-Labor with God

Kenneth Hill

with Lanny Richardson

XULON PRESS

Xulon Press
2301 Lucien Way #415
Maitland, FL 32751
407.339.4217
www.xulonpress.com

© 2021 by Kenneth Hill

Contribution by Lanny Richardson

All rights reserved solely by the author. The author guarantees all contents are original and do not infringe upon the legal rights of any other person or work. No part of this book may be reproduced in any form without the permission of the author.

Due to the changing nature of the Internet, if there are any web addresses, links, or URLs included in this manuscript, these may have been altered and may no longer be accessible: The views and opinions shared in this book belong solely to the author and do not necessarily reflect those of the publisher. The publisher therefore disclaims responsibility for the views or opinions expressed within the work.

For more information, email ... info@parablesmedia.com

Unless otherwise indicated, Scripture quotations taken from the King James Version (KJV) – *public domain.*

Scripture quotations taken from the Holy Bible, New Living Translation (NLT). Copyright ©1996, 2004, 2007 by Tyndale House Foundation. Used by permission of Tyndale House Publishers, Inc.

Scripture quotations taken from the Holy Bible, New International Version (NIV). Copyright © 1973, 1978, 1984, 2011 by Biblica, Inc.™. Used by permission. All rights reserved.

Paperback ISBN-13: 978-1-66283-534-6
Ebook ISBN-13: 978-1-66283-556-8

Get Your FREE Gift

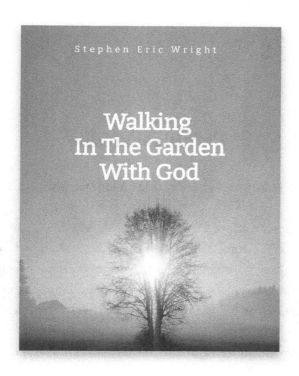

To get the best experience with this book, I've found readers who download and use ***Walking In The Garden With God*** are able to implement faster and take the next steps needed to co-laboring with God.

Get Your FREE Gift by visiting:
www.parablesmedia.com

Parables Media

Welcome to The Parables Media Community

Before you begin reading this book, Parables Media has created a Thank
You & Welcome Video we would like to share with you.
We are dedicated to bringing life to the stories of others like yourself who
long to have impact for the Kingdom of God in their spheres of influence.
You can access this video now by going to www.parablesmedia.com

Look for the *Welcome to The Parables Media Community* tab

Parables Media

Acknowledgements

There are times during the routine, seemingly mundane moments of our lives, that we have a profound impact on others. I know this to be true from my personal experience and gleanings from two phenomenal leaders. My life and legacy have been shaped by the examples of Mr. Frank Blake, former CEO of The Home Depot Inc. and Dr. Creflo Dollar, senior pastor of World Changers Church International.

I benefitted personally from Mr. Blakes' servant leadership style and his chosen team of leaders. Frank's generosity and concern for the people who worked in the stores was remarkable. I could provide countless examples of how his leadership benefited hourly associates. The team of leaders that emerged from Frank's staff reads like a Who's Who of CEO's: Craig Meneer (The Home Depot), Carol Tome (United Parcel Service), Marvin Ellison (Lowes, JC Penney), Hal Lawton (Tractor Supply, Macys). I don't know of many leaders who have produced a roster of this magnitude. I have been profoundly impacted Mr. Blake and his team. I am grateful to them for investing their time and concern into my career.

Dr. Creflo Dollar taught me many lessons. I benefitted greatly from his patient and detailed approach to teaching God's Word. It seemed as if he would teach on the same subject for weeks, as if he were waiting for me to grasp it. For example, when he began the teachings on love, they continued for a year. This was exactly what I needed. To have these teachings available during my struggles was an answered prayer. Observing him provided learnings, just as revisiting his sermon recordings have. His example of consistent excellence over decades reflects perseverance and character. I learned to face adversity with dignity and resolve from his example.

My professional and spiritual life have been impacted greatly by these leaders.

DEDICATION

This book is dedicated to the women and men of my life.

My wife, Clarisa, is my love and continues to amaze and refresh me with her grace, dedication, and wisdom. My mother, Gloria, who I could fill every page in this book with stories of her faith, hope, and love. My daughters, Zoe and Zuriel, who are blossoming into their own before my eyes. My mother in-law, Clara Collins has become a treasure in my life. To Doris Fuller and Sonya Reid who know my heart for them.

To the fathers who I love and affectionately think of as my forefathers. Robert Coatie, Lawrence Hill, John Thomas, and Edward Wilson, have each played a role in my life as only God could orchestrate. The full impact of their presence is still being realized which will require a separate book to unpack. Some left prematurely, while others answered the call to step in and fill the gap. God used this patchwork of earthly fathers to provide a glimpse of His perfect Fatherhood. His perfection compared to their limitations and His consistent presence contrasted with their seasons of absence, paints the picture of God providing all my needs.

Without question, the impact of Edward Wilson adopting me forever changed my life. Without any requirement or responsibility for me, he loved and invested in me as if his life depended on it. He availed the full extent of his resources to impact every area of my life. Edward Wilson provided as much healing to my orphaned heart as was humanly possible. Through his tangible example of love, I gained perception of

God's willingness to love and adopt me as a son. Dad looked past my flaws and saw my potential; he looked beyond my limitations and saw a legacy. As I look into the eyes of my children, I understand the hope that he had for me. Experiencing this unconditional love from God and man has galvanized my drive to elevate the underserved and to champion the cause for the forgotten. I am compelled to reach those who have been pushed aside or to the rear, and to let the common among us know that they are loved with an uncommon love.

To the cloud of witnesses that I have not mentioned by name. You know who you are: my siblings, relatives, coworkers, mentors, co-laborers in Christ and friends.

Grace and peace be multiplied to you.

Kenny

TABLE OF CONTENTS

FOREWORD

Psalm 127:1-2 says, "Unless the LORD builds the house, they labor in vain who build it; Unless the LORD guards the city, the watchman stays awake in vain. It is vain for you to rise up early, to sit up late, to eat the bread of sorrows; for so He gives His beloved sleep." (NKJV)

Kenneth Hill has spent the better part of his life understanding the truth of that Bible verse. For most of us the journey to freedom from a wrong view of work and calling can be a long and painful process. And some never learn those lessons.

When I read the manuscript of Kenneth's book, I read a story of a man who thought he knew how to succeed in his career at Home Depot but stumbled many times along the way. However, each stumble and failure, unknowingly to him, was a stepping-stone to a greater truth. And greater freedom.

Years ago, I wrote a book called Change Agent. In that book I discovered that many leaders I studied in the Bible all went through 6 stages to fulfill their calling. I recognized these 6 stages in Kenneth's journey.

Stage 1 is Recruitment through Crisis. Every leader God uses He allows a crisis in their life as the front door to their larger story in life. Kenneth was led into several crisis events in his 30-year journey at Home Depot. Little would he realize those crisis events were actually the door to experience his larger story.

Stage 2 is Character Development. God takes that leader through a series of painful lessons designed to mature that leader, often through his failures. Kenneth vulnerably shares his failures and what he learned from those failures to allow him to move toward his goal of success at Home Depot.

Stage 3 is Isolation. God sets the leader aside for a season to allow him to experience a mess in his life and to receive a message from God. That message transcends into a leader to become a messenger for God's purposes. Kenneth reveals how his own time of isolation led him to discover new messages from God for himself.

Stage 4 is the Cross. I observed that almost every leader had some form of betrayal in their life. That betrayal is God's graduate level course for leadership. Moses experienced it. King David experienced it. Jesus experienced it. Jesus said that we must forgive those who wrong us, or He will not forgive us. In fact, He said we are to *bless* our enemies. Kenneth shares how he experienced betrayal in his own life and what God taught him in that betrayal.

Stage 5 is the Problem-Solving stage. Every leader God uses is a problem solver. He created us to be problem solvers. Culture does not care who solves their problem, they just want their problem solved. If you can solve a problem for someone or your employer, you become more valuable to that person or employer. Kenneth demonstrated that tangibly to his superiors at Home Depot.

Stage 6 is Networks. God uses networks of people to collaborate to achieve greater results through their collaboration. William Wilberforce collaborated with about 18 individuals in England who abolished slavery and 69 other world-changing initiatives. Kenneth learned how to serve his Home Depot team members to achieve success.

ELEVATED: My journey to co-labor with God is Kenneth's true story of these 6 stages in Kenneth's life. You will get to know Kenneth as he shares his failures, discoveries, and lessons that you will be able to apply in your own life. His 30-year career at Home Depot allows us to go inside the world of Home Depot, the challenges he faced and the lessons he learned. I related to so many of his stories and his conclusions.

Kenneth is no longer at Home Depot but is now in the second half of his life-long journey. What he learned in the first half is allowing him to build on those lessons for greater impact as a social entrepreneur and philanthropist.

Sit down with your coffee and this book and get to know Kenneth through the pages of his exceptional life story. It's one of those books you won't want to stop reading to learn what new lessons are to follow in the next pages and chapters.

Os Hillman - Founder and President of Marketplace Leaders www.marektplaceleaders.org

International Leader on Faith and Work. Author of 18 books and TGIF Today God Is First – www.todaygodisfirst.com - Daily devotional that is read throughout the world.

INTRODUCTION

On May 7, 2015, I boarded a flight to Chicago to appear as a guest on the nationally syndicated Steve Harvey television show. I was invited to represent The Home Depot for a Father's Day special presentation.

As I found my seat on the plane, I started thinking about my career and all the great things that happened to me the last 15 years of my 30-year career with The Home Depot.

I was handpicked as The Home Depot Representative for the Steve Harvey radio show for over four years. I was assigned to assist Mr. Harvey's Summer Camp for young men. I participated in a multicity tour, promoting the "Do it Herself" Workshop Series with Steve Harvey. And I was granted VIP access to the Annual Steve Harvey Neighborhood Awards events in Las Vegas, New York, and Atlanta. These opportunities were just one aspect of God's blessings experienced in my career as I embraced the journey to co-labor with Him.

Inside the pages of this book, you will read the story of two different careers in every way imaginable. Ultimately, I succeeded and experienced a career beyond my expectations.

While there were some business and leadership principles that I employed, the principles themselves are not the reason for my success. My success was the result of God's elevation in my life as my relationship with Him shifted from being estranged to fully dedicated to this essential relationship.

All the rewards, recognition, and compensation were the result of my surrender to follow God's principled journey of how-to co-labor with Him in every aspect of my life.

These principles will work for anyone and every time. Regardless of your field of industry, your level of skill or ability, or how dire the circumstances you are facing.

I invite you to come along in the pages of this book and understand how God is inviting you to co-labor with Him as you learn how to receive His instructions, rely on His strength to carry them out and experience His nature.

For His Renown,
Kenneth Hill

> *"You will live in joy and peace. The mountains and the hills will burst into song, and the tress of the field will clap their hands! Where once there were thorns, cypress trees will grow. Where nettles grew, myrtles will sprout up. These events will bring great renown to the LORD's name; they will be an everlasting sign of His power and love." — Isaiah 55:12-13 NLT*

MY ISSUES

"Guard your heart above all else, for it determines the course of your life." — *Proverbs 4:23 NLT*

LEVEL 1

MY IMAGE CONFUSION

I tried earnestly for the first fifteen years of my career to achieve success and significance. I tried to build something that I could feel proud of only to fail. That's right, my career with The Home Depot spanned thirty years and the first fifteen of those years I would describe as utter frustration. The Bible has another word for it, it's called "toil."

> *"It is in vain that you rise early and go late to rest, eating the bread of anxious toil." — Psalm 127:2*

For fifteen years the bread of anxious toil was my steady diet. During that time, I tried everything in my power to create career success. I wanted nothing more than to promote and advance myself. I focused intensely on my performance. I arrived early to work. I stayed late. I did everything I thought I could to get ahead. I would work overtime to finish projects and keep my department up to standard. When I could no longer work overtime, I would clock out and continue to work "off the clock."

My focus on performance only led to frustration. The more I relied on what I was accomplishing, the fewer people seemed to notice. When I felt my efforts were not recognized, I would become depressed. During my bouts of depression, my performance dropped. I ended up going through a cycle from high performance with seemingly no progress towards promotion, to depression, and low performance. Eventually, I would receive some form of external motivation and then climb back to high performance.

The external motivation usually came from someone who was experiencing success in his or her career. It was often a friend or college classmate who shared how their career was developing. During college, my classmates and I measured our GPA against one another. Now in the workplace, measuring career success was the new badge of honor. Working as an hourly associate during college was perfectly acceptable for me. However, after graduation, I needed something to show for the years of experience and the degree I had earned. During these conversations, I would be asked "Are you still with The Home Depot? Are you a manager, yet?" The conversation would usually end with "I love shopping at your stores."

Hearing those words were bittersweet. I loved the fact that people liked shopping at the place that I worked. It meant we were doing something right and I was a part of it. In social settings, people would introduce themselves to me and say, "I hear you work for The Home Depot." They would continue by sharing a project experience or ask a question. When the discussion turned to my role in the company, the conversation hit a sour note within me. I would leave those conversations with a determination to make The Home Depot, not only a great place for people to shop, but a great career opportunity for myself. This led back to my performance orientation which fueled my depression cycle.

Because I worked while I was going to college, in my mind, I had checked all the boxes to achieve success. I had several years of experience, and I completed my degree with solid performance evaluations. However, things were not working as I expected. While I accumulated a small fortune of company stock during the years as I worked my way through college, I should have been content to be patient and wait for my opportunity. Yet, I couldn't wait or be patient because other people around me were being promoted. Something was missing in my life.

I thought it was the promotion, the title, and status that came with it. But there was more missing than a promotion. I was feeling rejected, a familiar experience that I thought earning a degree, and having a size-able stock portfolio would have resolved.

Rejection was introduced into my life as a child. I faced feelings of abandonment early in my life. I was raised by a single mother who did all that she could for my siblings and me. We never went to bed hungry or ran out of clean clothes to wear. On occasion, our dad would call and say to mom, "I'm going to pick the kids up and keep them this weekend." When those calls came, my mom would be excited that our dad wanted to spend time with us. She would share the news with excitement that dad was coming this weekend to pick us up. Our anticipation was so strong. So much so, we floated on air the rest of the week. We sang and danced on the way to school. We drew pictures and made cards to give daddy. We wondered where he would take us. Our favorite place was going to the Pizza Parlor. We had visions of all the great things that were going to happen. We looked forward to spending time with daddy and telling him all the things we were learning in school. It was not often that he called and even more rare for him to come and pick us up.

On the weekend that daddy was to come pick us up, we all got up Saturday morning in a flurry not even wanting to eat breakfast. We cleaned up our rooms and got dressed. Our little bags of clothes would already be packed, and we would be sitting on the front porch waiting for daddy to come. I remember waiting and talking about all the fun we were finally about to experience. One hour passed and there was still no sight of dad and no phone call. Two hours passed and still no news. Eventually mom would say, "You all come on in here and get some breakfast." Frowns flashed across our faces for a moment. We were hoping daddy would take us to breakfast. Nevertheless, we were hungry. So, we sat at the table still talking about the great things that could happen.

By lunchtime, mom would start calling daddy with no answer. Our dream weekend started to fade away. We cried and asked our mom why he didn't show up. It would take her the rest of the weekend to comfort us and convince us that he would come another time and make up for it. It was disappointing for us and had to be hard on her to see us hurt. She finally stopped telling us when he said he was coming. As much as I loved him, something made me feel that we were not good enough or important enough for his time. That same feeling of not enough followed me everywhere including my job.

This type of childhood disappointment tore a hole in my heart. I was trying to fill the lack of acceptance and approval with promotion and status at work. Then, when my career seemed to be in a holding pattern, I started to buy things to make me feel better. Before long, I had run through most of my stock portfolio, purchasing things my salary could not afford. Because of this financial irresponsibility, I now needed a promotion to get my finances back on track. The hole in my heart wasn't any closer to being filled or healed by gaining things. The feeling of not measuring up crept into every area of my life. An emptiness that would not go away clouded my thinking and led to numerous poor decisions.

I grew up in the church, literally attending three to four services a week. The congregation was a close-knit, loving group who became extended family. The church provided my mother the support and teaching she needed to manage single parenthood. My early impression of God was of someone who demanded strict adherence to rules and regulations. I accepted Christ when I was ten years old. As I grew, I became more aware of my inability to adhere to all the rules I was taught to pleased Him. I remember hearing over and over "it's better to be hot or cold. If you are lukewarm, God will spit you out of His mouth." Listening to the demands of the people around me, I did not know how I could measure up to such a standard. I knew God was real and I did not want to be offensive to him. I rationalized that I was better off leaving God alone, rather than trying to measure up and failing miserably.

It's amazing to think that I was convinced that if I would just get my promotion everything would be fine. I didn't select this strategy completely on my own. This was the working model I saw in management, every day. Hourly associates without a degree worked hard, stayed late, did whatever it took, and they soon received promotions. Hourly Supervisors who were promoted to Salaried Managers typically received a company stock award along with lucrative stock options that could be exercised in the future. These were life-changing opportunities. I often thought, "Why wasn't this strategy working for me?" My performance reviews were always good but not good enough to elevate me to the next level.

> *"Unless the Lord builds the house, they labor in vain that build it. Unless the Lord watches the city, the watchman stays awake in vain. It is in vain that you rise early and go late to rest, eating the bread of anxious toil." — Psalm 127:1-2*

Through this experience, I developed an understanding of this truth. Unless the Lord builds the career, the business, the marriage, whatever you are trying to accomplish, everything is in vain.

The Bread of Anxious Toil

Psalm 127 mentions eating the bread of anxious toil. Toil means exhausting physical labor or to work extremely and incessantly hard. Hard work was not new to me. I grew up as the eldest of seven siblings in a single-parent household. By the age of ten, I was able and expected to cook, clean the table, wash dishes, do the laundry, and always watch my brothers and sisters.

We lived in housing projects on the West side of Fresno, California. Walking to school each morning was a revelation of the crime and adult activity that had occurred during the night before. On several occasions, gun battles broke out on the way home from school. I remember my mother sternly telling me, "You make sure that your brothers and sisters make it home, even if you don't."

Fresno is located in the Central Valley region of California. This San Joaquin Valley is known as the "breadbasket of the nation", the agricultural capital of the region. By the time I was twelve years old, I spent every summer working in the fields, harvesting grapes, watermelons, plums, and peaches. Field work is labor-intensive during hot summer days. I learned what hard work was and it did not bother me. I learned to like it. Despite the hard work, I felt like I had accomplished something. I enjoyed that feeling and the paycheck that helped my mother.

When I turned fifteen, I applied for a job at McDonald's. The labor law required you to be sixteen to work as a minor, so I forged the date on my birth certificate and applied. The available position was during the lunchtime rush. Although I hoped to work weekends and evenings, this was my only opportunity to work. Therefore, I dropped my elective classes at school, packed my uniform in my bookbag, and rode the bus to work every day. The pace was fast, and the grill was hot. However, it did not compare to eight-hour shifts in the scorching heat harvesting produce.

I learned to work hard at a young age and this type of work convinced me that I didn't want to work in the fields for the rest of my life. When I started with The Home Depot, I was a student at the University of California in San Diego. I was determined to complete the requirements for my degree. At the same time, The Home Depot was expanding rapidly in California. The company was looking for people to take leadership roles. My supervisors came to me on several occasions trying to convince me to quit school and focus on moving up with the company. One supervisor stated, "Kenny, you have what it takes. You can be a leader and move up in this company. We're growing fast. You can always go back to school." I liked the company. I liked helping people and the camaraderie with my coworkers. But I was committed to my college education. I was determined to finish my education and get my degree. Being the eldest of seven siblings, I wanted to be an example. I wanted them to see that a college degree was attainable. I continued to respectfully decline my supervisor's recruitment efforts.

Once I graduated, the company had entered a moderate growth phase, but the rapid pace of new store openings had leveled off. At this same time, I was looking for the opportunity to move ahead. I had obtained my degree and had several years of experience under my belt. Nothing was holding me back except now the opportunities were not there. If I had been willing to be patient and wait for the next growth stage, opportunities would have returned. Yet, I did not have the benefit of hindsight. I wasn't being patient. I didn't know how big the company would become or how many leadership careers would be available. It was frustrating being told to wait, so I decided that I was going to make it happen.

Therefore, I committed myself to excellent performance, but my anxiety level was stifling. I blamed myself for passing up the promotion opportunities while I was in college. People that I trained had been promoted and seemed to be thriving in their leadership roles. All around me were career examples of what should have been available to me. I continued to apply myself, I pushed with performance determined to create a promotion for myself. I was on a strict diet of the bread of anxious toil. I was experiencing the anxiety that accompanies someone trying to force something to happen in their career. Relying on my knowledge, strength, and connections, I was determined to make things work. Had I succeeded; it would have been attributed to my skills and work ethic, but my lack of success created self-doubt and constant questioning.

Image

After a while, I learned that performance alone was not enough to get me where I wanted to go. While it seemed to be working for others, there was something else I needed. I was determined to figure it out.

That's when I began to focus on my image. I had my college degree and I felt this is what would separate me from other people. I wanted to look the part and say the right things to show that I was an intelligent and thoughtful leader. I wanted to make sure that the people who were making decisions about my career had a great image of me as a leader.

Carrying the weight of a self-built image is hard work. I became super sensitive about what people said or thought about me. I would become so nervous when I was around members of the leadership team. This didn't create a comfortable environment for me or anyone around me. When I focused on image building, I tended to talk about myself a lot. These actions drove people away from me. It's embarrassing to think about some of the ways I acted during this time in my career. Being prideful was not my personality. Yet, I felt I had to become this way because the people being promoted were aggressive Type A personality leaders. Instead of being who I genuinely was, I tried to make myself into what I thought the company was looking for.

Networks and Exposure

"It's not what you know but who you know." I don't quite remember where I first heard this phrase. It may have been at work or possibly at school. But I do remember hearing it in both settings. On one occasion a coworker of mine came up and told me that one of the Supervisors in our store had just been promoted to the role of Assistant Manager. I was new to the company and still in school. I wasn't thinking about a promotion at that time, but my coworker was. So, I asked him, "How did that happen?" I was trying to figure out what the process was for a person to be promoted. I wasn't sure if it was seniority-based or some other criteria, so I was genuinely inquiring. He replied, "It's not always what you know but who you know."

The next time that I recall hearing this infamous phrase was at school. During my second year at UC San Diego, I took a filler class that was not required for my major but counted towards graduation. I ended up in the class with someone that I knew. The class was near the end of the quarter, and he was graduating. During one class, he pulled out an envelope and slid it to me. I opened it up and saw a letter. It was a job offer for him to start as soon as he graduated. I don't remember the company or the amount of the salary, but it was impressive at the time. I had heard about job offers and salary negotiations, but this was the first actual offer letter that I had ever seen. I thought to myself "How awesome it must feel to have a major company want you on their team and offer you a nice salary and vacation package from day one."

"How did you get this offer so soon?" I whispered to him. "It's not always what you know but who you know" he replied. I was so excited about his offer that I started sharing the news with other seniors that I knew. One of the guys approached my friend and I after class one day. He expressed his interest about the company and asked if there was an ongoing recruiting process.

My friend listened and then quickly replied that there was not an ongoing recruiting process but that he had a personal contact with someone at the company. While this comment ended our conversation, it was the beginning of my contemplation of the role of personal contacts in career development.

I had been taught from my childhood to work hard and let my work speak for itself. I was to be kind, respectful, and honest. I was taught that this would be enough. But I remember thinking, maybe this only works in my mother's world. She had never experienced the rigors and competitive environment of the University of California education system. Almost every student was near the top of their class in high school. They came from middle to upper-class homes where one or both parents had college degrees. I vividly remember thinking, maybe this was a different world with different rules.

Later that year I had a conversation about my career with a mentor. He told me that I should write the CEO of The Home Depot a letter. It sounded crazy to me at first. I thought, "Why would the CEO of a Fortune 500 company pay attention to a letter from a college student who worked as a part-time associate in the electrical department?" My mentor insisted and I told him that I would think about it. But I wasn't sure that I wanted to follow through. I felt it would be a waste of time and just maybe my supervisors and managers would find out and be upset? Then I remembered my friend and his job offer through a personal contact. I remembered thinking, "Maybe this was a part of the new world that I am discovering. Maybe this is how things get done." So, I wrote and rewrote the letter several times to Bernie Marcus, CEO of The Home Depot.

I saw both Bernie Marcus and Arthur Blank on the broadcasted store meeting videos held each month. I tried to imagine Bernie Marcus's face reading my letter. I hoped he wouldn't be frowning. My letter was brief, I talked about how much I had enjoyed being an Associate with the company and thanked him for the great work environment that he had created. I told him about my studies and upcoming graduation and asked for his advice on upcoming opportunities with the company.

I felt a sigh of relief when I mailed the letter thinking, "Ok I did it, but I'll never get a response." To my surprise, one month later, I received a letter from the office of Bernie Marcus, CEO of The Home Depot. I was shocked that Bernie Marcus had responded to my letter. I opened the envelope to find my original letter inside. As I opened it, I noticed that he had responded to my letter with these words, "Dear Kenneth, either give me a call directly or call Don McKenna. My congratulations on your degree, Bernie."

I couldn't believe my eyes. The CEO had taken the time to reply to me. I remember thinking to myself, "Is this the power of networking?" With one letter I was invited for a phone call with the CEO or his Vice President of Human Resources. My level of excitement was incredible. I made the phone calls and was set up with a meeting in Atlanta with Mr. McKenna. The expectations that I had for my career with the company couldn't be any higher. While I wasn't sure exactly what the next phase would look like, I knew my future was bright. As incredible as it seemed to me that Bernie Marcus responded to my letter, he showed me what a servant leader looks like.

I was excited for the meeting with Mr. McKenna, but it didn't live up to my expectations. I was looking forward to hearing about the opportunities to grow a career at the corporate office. With my store experience and a degree, I was sure that there would be a good fit. I arrived at the meeting in a business suit, as I was coached. Mr. McKenna welcomed me into his office and sat down at his desk. Suddenly I felt overdressed. He was wearing a pair of slacks and a dress shirt with the sleeves rolled up to his elbows. He looked at me for a while before he said anything. I felt like my appearance offended him. I started to ask if I could use the men's room and go take off my suit jacket and tie. Instead, I just sat there as he looked at me like I was from Mars. I was used to wearing casual clothes to work but for a meeting of this caliber, I wanted to make a good impression. Judging by the way he looked at me, that was a mistake. He told me that the growth of the company was in the stores and that is where I should be focused if I wanted to build a career. Just like that, the meeting was over. I could have kicked myself, afterwards. My focus on making a good impression had totally offended the Vice-President of Human Resources. This was yet another level of rejection that would torment me for years. I had the prime opportunity to leverage a connection and blew it. Yet, I didn't let the meeting stop me from moving to Atlanta. I was sure that something would eventually open up at the corporate office.

The dynamics of the company's growth at that time was exponential growth in California, Florida, and Texas. Yet, the Atlanta market where the company started has only grown from four stores to eight by the time I transferred. I left a division where new stores were popping up all over the place to arrive at a place that had limited growth. In California, there would often be multiple new stores opening at the same time. This created a huge need for talent to run these stores. Promotions came in waves and the company had to bring people from the Atlanta market to fill managerial positions in California.

From a pure career opportunity perspective, I would have been better off staying in San Diego for promotion. Instead, my focus was on an office job at the corporate office. Considering my peers and their job offers, I wanted something similar. I had enough experience with the way the stores operated and a college degree. I wanted more. Unfortunately, this plan never came to fruition. I interviewed but never received an offer from any of the corporate office positions.

My conversation with Mr. McKenna often came back to my mind as he described those opportunities in the stores were the wave of the future for the company. My networking strategy was not working as I expected, and I was still an hourly associate in the store searching for an opportunity. The harder I worked, the more I ate "the bread of anxious toil" and I was thinking this just might be my way of life, but I was driven to get more.

LEVEL 2

My Distorted Focus

When you face something negative or the unexpected occurs in your life, what is the tone of your mental conversation? What type of thoughts immediately go through your mind? For a long time in my life, I would dwell on the negative impacts of things that happened or didn't happen. I would immediately think, "This is bad. How am I going to deal with this? I am not going to make it and there is probably somebody working against me." I am embarrassed to admit that I allowed such terrible thoughts to permeate my thinking. Thankfully, this is no longer the case for me. I chose to learn that successful people learn to face challenges believing that a solution exists and that maybe an opportunity can be leveraged during troubled times. Training myself to respond to trials in a positive manner and eradicating negativity were huge steps that are worth sharing.

A great example of my need for a mindset change came when layoffs were announced for my position on the Loss Prevention Team. After recently being promoted and completing the training to be a part of this group, I had thoughts of "How am I going to make house payments? How am I going to make it? What is going to happen next?" As these thoughts flooded in, my mindset was on failure, fear, and loss.

With so many people potentially losing their jobs, there was a rush to find new opportunities and the Director of our department was concerned. Several team members had been in his department for years, but

I was the newest member of the team. While they had responded to his leadership and helped him achieve goals, I thought that he would work on behalf of those senior people and assist them in finding new roles but not me. I was surprised that he also came to me and expressed his commitment to assist me in finding other opportunities. He made calls and arranged opportunities for me to interview for open positions. This may seem like a small thing, but it was God intervening on my behalf and working through others to assist me.

The Bible is clear that we are responsible for controlling the thoughts that occupy space in our minds. Philippians 4:8 instructs us to think on things that are true, pure, lovely, excellent, and praiseworthy. We are also encouraged in Isaiah 26:3 that God will keep us in perfect peace if our minds are steadfast in trusting Him. We cannot keep negative thoughts from passing through our minds. However, when they come and become occupants, our focus shifts. This begins the process of meditation. What you meditate on is what you produce in your life. Meditation on negative things produces unwanted fruit. In contrast, meditating on God's promises will invite God to intervene.

As I look back at this situation, my mindset was on failure, fear, and loss. What God produced was the opposite. I interviewed and received an offer to become an Assistant Manager at the Cascade store. Therefore, I received a promotion and a raise.

In retrospect, the department reorganization positioned me on the path of my career mission. The plan that God had for the next 15 years of my career came on the heels of a perceived lay off. I have learned how God is always there for me. He is working behind the scenes for my good. This is what the Scripture means when it tells us to think on things that are good, pure, and of good report. Despite my negative meditation, God intervened on my behalf. This helped me to develop trust in God's love and concern for me. With an understanding of this love, my confidence in what He promises became stronger. I chose to make meditation on God's promises instead of negative possibilities more consistent in my daily life.

God had a specific plan and destiny for me that was connected to the Cascade store. I was focused on the circumstances impacting me, but God was planning and preparing me to be an impact on the lives of hundreds of associates and thousands of customers during my leadership tenure.

Problems are not unbeknownst to God. He is already working His plan for victory. Your success is already on God's mind. While it may not be a walk in the park, He has promised to walk with you and even to carry you if necessary.

> *"For I know the plans that I have for you declares the Lord, plans for well-being and not for calamity, in order to give you hope and a future." —Jeremiah 29:11*

Are you employed in the occupation of your choosing, or are you deployed in the marketplace for God's purposes? God has a specific purpose for you that requires your skillset and giftings. Taking the time to seek Him as a priority and being open to His direction will guide your steps. Your situation does not have to include facing potential job loss like I did. It is vitally important to ask that His will and purpose be fulfilled in your life and be open to accept it. His purpose for us will always be better than anything we can plan or construct on our own.

Being deployed for God's purpose led me to accept positions at the Cascade store on two different occasions. Much of my career assignment was tied to that specific location. I would not have chosen that particular store; however, God's plan was clear. I spent over ten years or a third of my career in this one store. At times, the challenges seemed insurmountable. There were days that I thought my career with the company was over, and there were a few times that I wished as much. All along, God was building and developing me as a leader. It would have been easier to spend ten years at a less challenging location and in a more comfortable environment. However, my experience galvanized my faith and confidence to face any challenge and succeed.

Being positioned at the Cascade store was not exclusively for my development. God wanted to use me to reach the associates and customers with a level of servant leadership that they had yet to experience. Many times, our assignments are for the benefit of the people He places us around. Our sphere of influence can be impacted by our example and lifestyle.

The situations and environments that redefine us create a vantage point for others to see God's handiwork in our lives. The level of love and kindness required to transform the Cascade store was not something that I had a grasp on when I arrived. It was developed in me over the years as people watched. As I relinquished my plans and accepted His will, my transformation became a message that words alone could not speak.

Soldiers do not get to choose the location of their deployment. They have little control over the length of time they are attached to a unit. This allows them to focus on executing the mission or function that they are given. Soldiers learn to trust and respect the leadership that they are under as the leadership assigns and deploys the proper support when and where it's needed. Too often our civilian mindsets cause us to spend time worrying or complaining about things that are in place for a reason.

Are you currently in a place that is challenging you and at times making you uncomfortable? Is your current situation causing you to pray for God's help and direction? People often distance themselves from situations of this type. It's proven that most growth and development occur during times of adversity and challenge. Are you running away from your true growth potential or praying that God will remove you from the refining fire? A change of perspective may be all the change that is needed. Once you accept the deployment order from your commander and chief you can begin the journey towards elevation.

LEVEL 3

My Crisis of Faith

After years of striving to achieve success in my career and marriage, I finally hit the wall, had the wind knocked out of me and had a meltdown. You name the cliché for the disaster, and it fit my situation. When everything around you falls apart, and when the things in which you trust the most fail, devastation lies before you.

I am not alone in experiencing this pain, because people, businesses, even nations often find themselves facing critical crises. I will show you how I found hope amidst the pain and carnage of my life. Circumstances beyond my control and pain seemingly beyond my ability to endure birthed purpose and strategy that transformed my life.

Devastation was happening all around me. My career had turned into an impossible situation. My marriage was suffocating. Facing these challenges at the same time would cause some people to give up hope and turn to self-destructive behavior. This was the most difficult time of my life. My faith was being greatly tested. I was actively serving at my church. I was doing all that I knew to be a good husband. I was giving one hundred and ten percent on my job. The harder I tried the worse things seem to become.

My Career

Following the reorganization of my department, I was promoted to Assistant Manager. My new store was one of the most challenging stores in the company. The Cascade store is located in Historic Southwest Atlanta, which was home to distinguished residents including: the late Hank Aaron, H. J. Russell, Congressman John Lewis, and former Mayor Maynard Jackson. This community also includes Andrew Young, former Atlanta Mayor Shirley Franklin, and many more influential African American leaders, professional athletes, and entertainers. The area boasts some of the finest homes in the region. Yet, among those very established and middle-class families, the disenfranchised poor were sprinkled throughout the area. The Cascade store did not successfully serve this diverse customer base. The most influential customers usually opted to shop at a different store location, rather than encounter the store's low standards.

Furthermore, the high incidence of crime in the area also led to the stress and complications of managing the store. Cars were routinely burglarized or stolen from the parking lot. I remember once having a car stolen every day of the week. Unfortunately, most of them belonged to associates. Also, for many years, the company policy allowed cash refunds without a receipt. If you bought something from The Home Depot and it didn't work out, you could return it for a full cash refund. While this provided great customer service for most of our customers, it also provided an opportunity for dishonest people. Thieves would steal merchandise and bring it back to receive cash. A whole industry of theft rings with coordinated efforts across several states was created. Needless to say, the Cascade store was the epicenter of the scamming.

All cash refunds over a certain dollar amount required a manager to approve the transaction. Far too often, a manager would essentially spend his shift at the customer returns desk. Refusing to approve a refund for a customer would often get ugly. During the era of the crack cocaine epidemic, drug users used stolen merchandise to pay for their habits. Stealing product from the shelves or from behind the building was a daily routine. Recognizing the stressful and dangerous work conditions, the company hired off-duty police to patrol certain stores. Yes, the Cascade store made the list.

Profitability was a sore topic for the store as well. Associate and customer accidents, employee theft, lack of morale, and poor customer service contributed to declining productivity. High turnover rates with associates and the management team became the norm. Employees with career aspirations quickly transferred to a different store or left the company. Store leadership often looked for quick fix remedies for the most pressing problems instead of laying a foundation for sustained success. Nevertheless, there was a core group of associates and supervisors who loved the store and the community it served.

This small group of committed souls added tremendous value and kept things moving forward. They went above and beyond without being asked. The remaining associates consisted of people who showed up to do just enough to receive a paycheck. New associates were always impacted by these two groups. There was a tug of war to draw the new people to join one side or the other. The negative message usually won and the hope for positive change would fade.

These types of issues were directly or indirectly impacted by leadership. The company needed to see improvement and some consistent performance. The General Manager position had been a revolving door for several years. Leaders rarely developed the people in the building. These huge performance gaps eventually carried over to the store's physical appearance.

During the 1998 NFL season, the Atlanta Falcons made a run to the Superbowl. The team adopted the name "The Dirty Birds." I believe it was a play on the term "Dirty South" that local rap artists Goodie Mob made popular. The company assigned a location number to identify stores. During this time, the Cascade store became known as "The Dirty 130." From trash littered through the parking lot, to aisles crowded with carts of return merchandise, the appearance was a disaster. The store restrooms, associate breakroom, and the training room, all reflected apathy, disarray, and disregard. It was an embarrassment for anyone to be associated with the Cascade store, especially when attending regional training events.

Adding these stress points to an already demanding job narrowed the field of managerial candidates. The type of leader that was typically assigned to the store was a thick skinned, stern, non-negotiable Type-A personality. Leaders that didn't have an affinity towards listening and developing people would burn-out themselves and the associates. The cycle continued for years ending with the same results and the store not being any closer to what the associates and the community deserved. For example, on my first day at Cascade, the majority of the Assistant Managers were transferred to other stores or terminated from the company. I operated with the understanding that failing to transform this location could mean the end of my career as well.

On top of all this, my marriage was failing. My wife wanted her freedom. The cause of which I attributed to the lack of finances and career success. Even while I was home, I was faced with the consequences of my failing career. I found myself questioning, "What did I do to deserve this? Why am I in this position after all I've tried to do? Why am I in such a terrible place?" Of course, I didn't think it was fair. Other people around me were experiencing success. I had trained several people who had received promotions, but it was not working for me. I tried diligently to treat my wife like my queen and never thought I would face divorce. I had been a hard worker, a faithful husband, and a devoted believer. I believed I had checked all the boxes to have success in my life. Yet everything was crashing down around me. I had to accept the reality that I didn't have the answers and everything I thought I knew was useless.

Purpose Found

Serving in the youth ministry at my church had become a place of calm in my otherwise stormy life. I had served in Youth Ministry for several years. I enjoyed it and felt like I was making a difference. The team made me feel needed and the youth respected me and even sought me out for advice.

I needed change in my life, and I was praying. Yet, I was not receiving any direction. I was thinking, "Should I forget about my career with The Home Depot and go in a different direction?" As I pondered a career change, my church posted a job opening in the Youth Ministry. Immediately, I thought to myself, "Was this the answer to my prayers?" I became so excited at the thought of trading in my stress filled days at the store for Full-time Youth Ministry. I knew there would be a difference in salary, but I was confident that I would figure that out, later.

When I interviewed, the Ministry Leadership said, "We'd be glad to have you." I thought, "Great, this is my way out." I wasn't concerned about anything else other than an escape from my current situation. At the end of the interview, the Director said, "You go home and pray about it. Come back and let us know." Honestly, I had already settled that it was a done deal before I left the interview.

But, when I went home and started thinking about praying, I didn't get a chance to pray. I was planning to remind God about everything I had been through and all that I had suffered. As I rehearsed my strategic plan, God spoke to my heart and said, "Your job is your mission field." I knew it was God because that was not the response that I wanted to hear. Furthermore, I didn't have mission field on my mind. I replied, "Lord, poor people in Africa and China need missionaries. These people I work with have heard of Jesus and the Gospel. They are simply choosing not to respond to your invitation of salvation." He calmly replied, "Yes, they may have heard about me but now I want someone to show them. I want them to see and experience love at work. They need to see a Christ-centered Servant Leader. "

The answer left me deflated because I thought I had found my exit. I perceived that I was finally getting relief in one area of my life. But now I had been recommissioned. I was being invited to focus on my workplace as my mission field. Looking back, I wish I had engaged in more conversation with God. I really needed more detailed instructions on how and what this assignment involved. Unfortunately, I assumed that I already knew and so off I went into the mission field.

In a literal foreign mission field, a missionary learns about the culture, performs acts of service to demonstrate the love of God, and then shares about God. I began to strategize how I could accomplish this professionally. It was encouraging and somewhat refreshing to know that I belonged and found purpose at my job. The problems didn't disappear, but hope had been birthed in me. My hope was redirected to impact the lives of my associates. God adjusted my focus towards helping others and inspired the possibility of better things to come.

My Marriage

On the home scene, my wife delivered her departing address. We had not been living as a normal couple for a long time. We had two separate bedrooms and rarely had conversations that extended beyond hello. We lived like roommates who needed each other to pay the rent and utilities. I was patiently awaiting change in our marriage. I had exhausted all my solutions. We went to counseling sessions. While it helped me understand some areas of our relationship, it didn't seem to change her mind. She wanted out and I was trying to hold onto her and our marriage. I felt that all the struggle in my life would eventually end, and I adamantly wanted her present to rejoice with me. She still declared, "I'm leaving."

I cried out to God for help in all my despair. I was desperate and felt that it was not fair. Considering all that I had invested, I did not understand why I was experiencing this level of destruction in my marriage. We attended conferences to learn our roles as husband and wife. We studied the Bible together, prayed together, and dreamed of what our lives would become. I never imaged it would come to this. Somewhere along the line, the constant financial pressure had injured her. I didn't like the situation we were in, but I was facing the challenge hoping for the day that things would change. Our situation impacted her differently. It was as though she had been stretched beyond her limit, like a garment that had been pulled so far out of shape that it loses the ability to return to its original form. She once repeated the scripture to me "Hope deferred makes the heart sick." The exposure to the elements that I had allowed had made her sick. She was sick of waiting for things to get better and sick of wishing things were different. My bad financial decisions and failures hurt her. She was injured and no longer concerned if her actions hurt me.

Two major areas in my life erupted into chaotic uncertainty. I did not know what the future held. I did not foresee how being a missionary to my job was going to work or even what it looked like. Just as the promise of purpose began to shine through the debris covering my life, my wife moved out of the house. The crises in my life were fully developed, raging storms. I wish I could say I knew all along that I would make it. My circumstances challenged everything that I knew and everything I believed in. I continually asked myself "What's wrong with me? Why isn't anything working? Why can't I do anything right?"

My only source of comfort was that God would never leave me nor forsake me. I had convinced myself that I had done something wrong to end up in such a desolate condition. I could not identify what it was, but I believed this did not just happen without reason. A voice in my head screamed, "You're never going to recover from this. Give up! You're an embarrassment as a follower of Christ." I was dubious as to how I would emerge from these circumstances. I knew for certain that God accepted people buried under all types of debris and rubble. Since I already belonged to Him, I could only hope that He saw my condition and would not leave me destitute.

Suddenly, in a moment, my life had crumbled into total chaos. Like a house of cards hit by hurricane force winds, my finances, career, and marriage lay in a tangled and twisted mess. I found myself lying on the floor of our empty house, crying a puddle into the carpet. I was hurt, angry, and embarrassed all at the same time. I surrendered knowing that I had no other options. I had no back up plan. I was bankrupt of human possibilities for recovery. I cried out to God and told him "This is not fair. It is not right. I do not deserve this. You can't leave me like this. Tell me what I did wrong or tell me what to do."

Out of my cry of despair, God spoke calmly; "Love is the answer." I thought about my mistreatment at work and home, and I shouted, "Love doesn't have anything to do with what I'm going through, God." Again, God calmly replied; "Love gives." I thought about my lack of finances and how hard I had been working to get relief. I replied, "I don't have anything to give." It was at that moment that God made it crystal clear. He spoke three small words that changed my life, forever. I asked God to tell me what to do to change my situation, but he was telling me who to become. I wanted an explanation and retribution for what I was going through, but He was focused on where I was headed and who I was becoming. He simply replied, "Kindness is free." I remember thinking to myself, "Could it really be that simple? Can love and kindness change the mess that I am in?"

I thought of the Bible story in 2 Kings 5:8-13 where Naaman the Syrian commander was told by Elisha the prophet to do a simple act in order to be cleansed of leprosy. The commander scoffed to his servant that he could dip into one of the rivers in his own country that were superior to the Jordan. His servant encouraged him to respond to the word of the Lord with obedience. Finally, Naaman surrendered and obeyed and was cleansed of his leprosy. At the same time, my mind was telling me "That's too simple, that works in church, but this is the real world." I began to ask myself some internal questions like, "Would I act on the instructions that I had received? Would I allow doubt to steal the instruction for my life? Or Would I continue to try to make it on my own?" The fact is, I had run out of solutions and was willing to listen no matter how simplistic the directions seemed. Even still, deep inside my mind and heart, I wondered if something so simple could provide the transformation that my life needed.

God had given Naaman instructions to receive a miracle. His leprosy disappeared instantly upon his obedience. God had given me instruction to change me from the inside out. I was wearing poverty and shame like a cloak. God was asking me to trust Him to experience the miraculous changes He had for my life, and it began with total surrender. That day lying on the carpet of my empty house, I gave in and surrendered. I had tried and failed for years. I died to myself and making it my way. I wasn't going to be able to accept the credit for anything good that came to me from here on out.

LEVEL 4

My Heart Transplant

After receiving instructions to base my life on love and kindness, I felt like a student retaking a course or repeating a grade. I thought I was nicer than most people and considerate of others' feelings. Given the degree of pain I endured from my marriage, I thought I was doing the love walk reasonably well. Nevertheless, I began to make it my focus to be intentionally kind. I determined to be helpful to everyone in my sphere of influence. My workplace was my mission field. Love and compassion were the tools I was to use. During the same time my pastor began teaching on a series on love for several months.

> *"Do nothing out of selfish ambition or vain conceit. Instead, in humility, value others above yourselves." — Philippians 2:3*

His teachings revealed things about love that I had forgotten and some that I had never considered. He emphasized the connection between love and trust. It is impossible to love without trust. The degree of confidence that we place in a person or relationship determines the depth of our love. God wants us to trust in Him and in His love for us. Nothing communicates our love for him more than complete trust. Selfishness, and self-preservation are the opposites of the love that is built on trust. Love leads us to trusting in God's ability to provide for and protect us. I thought about how I tried to defend myself in my marriage and provide for my career. It became natural to put up guards to keep people from hurting me. However, I learned that trusting God to defend me enabled me to remain focused on loving others. I needed to relearn love and its designed role in my life.

My pastor also talked about the importance of taking self out of the center of the focus of my life. Jesus endured pain and sorrow for us. Instead of becoming absorbed with the injustice of His situation, He turned His suffering into the ultimate display of love. He laid down His life for us.

Jesus considered us His friends, not because we were friendly towards Him, but because we needed Him. He is our only way out. Furthermore, as Christ was dying on the cross, He prayed for God to forgive those crucifying Him. He exemplifies showing concern for others and trusting God to take care of Him.

> "Greater love has no one than this: to lay down one's life for one's friends." — John 15:13

Through this Love series, I was reminded of the call to present my body a living sacrifice (Romans 12:2). This truth is not talking about a literal sacrifice because Jesus already did that on our behalf. But we are instructed to follow Christ's example and remain focused on the condition of others, despite our discomforts. Our acquaintance with pain and sorrow should result in our being more compassionate towards others. It was challenging to stop putting my concerns first. The issues of my life were trying to dominate my mind. I had to remind myself that God cared for me and trust that He was intervening on my behalf.

I began meditating on this more complete concept of love. By trusting that God loved me, I could focus on loving others. I found scriptures and wrote them on note cards. I took the note cards with me everywhere I went. I read them during my lunch break. I even wrote one of my favorite scriptures on the inside of my Home Depot apron. I would often read it and encourage myself during my shift.

I felt like I was still beneath a mountain of rubble, but, for the first time; I had the tools to dig my way out. Rays of light began to shine through as I grasped the essence of love and its power to transform. Furthermore, I was forging onward on a mission.

The fruit of the Spirit is love. Love anchors the remaining attributes which manifest in our lives. Love is the way into God's presence and the exit from harmful situations. Believing that God loved me unconditionally despite what I was going through was not automatic. I had to train myself to remember that what I was going through had not changed His love for me. My mistakes did not move the needle off of a "fully loved" status. His passion for me was consistent and consuming. It covered all my mistakes and inabilities.

Because of Christ's love for me, He desired to spend time with me. He wanted me to share my hurts and deepest desires with Him. My wife, family, and friends were focusing on their lives and other things. God, however, was available and wanted me to spend time with Him. Spending time reading the Bible and in prayer helped me focus on His love for me.

Time spent in His presence began to strengthen me. My confidence was growing roots. As I believed that He was working on my behalf, a hope emerged that I would recover the losses suffered in my finances and relationship. I began trusting that He was empowering me to impact my workplace. A change of perspective was rebuilding me from the inside. There was no external evidence that anything was happening. My life circumstances were the same, but I was changing. I was receiving an understanding of the depth of His love and concern for every detail of my life. As God filled me with His love, it overflowed into my approach and interactions with others.

Kindness is Free

Love is a precious commodity and kindness is its currency. As I accepted the deposit of His love into my heart, kindness began to flow towards others. I began to show kindness to anyone in my path. I recommitted myself to helping the associates at work. I became invested in their interests, not just as it related to work, but in their day-to-day lives. I wanted to know about their plans and dreams for their families. I inquired about their children, what they wanted to become and how I might help them? I was interested in knowing if there was something that The Home Depot could train them in their job to help in another area of their lives? Several associates had higher education desires. Some aspired to become business owners. I offered to show my associates how The Home Depot could teach them how to run a business. I trained myself to listen to people, to hear where and how I could help them. I remembered the problems they shared with me, and I prayed for them.

Walking in love and showing kindness transformed my interactions with customers as well. The Home Depot culture was to greet each customer with a smile and make eye contact as I welcomed them to the store. Now, I would ask their name and listened to their reason for shopping that day. I would remember their names and greet them by name on their next visit. As I walked them to the items they were looking for, I treated them like royalty. I thought of it as a "Royal Walk." The same level of attention that a dignitary or high-ranking official would receive was available to my customers. I noticed the details of their clothing and appearance and would give them a genuine compliment as we walked. I remembered previous conversations and asked follow-up questions. Reflecting on their sports teams, where they were from, the college or university they attended were all standard aspects of the "Royal walk."

The "Royal Walk" is the kind of service and interaction expected when someone was shopping for a new car or a house. I provided the same experience for someone purchasing a light bulb, an air filter, or a bag of plant food. My goal was to give them an experience that they would think about the rest of the day. After showing them their product options, I would ask to make sure they had the tools required to install the item. I would often continue to find the remaining items on their list or introduce them to one of my associates with instructions to take excellent care of them. If the customer purchased something large, heavy, or bulky; I offered to load it into their vehicle after purchasing it. Customers would say, "You don't have to do that" or "You're a manager, get somebody else to help me," to which I would reply, "That's why I'm here." Some customers were not sure how to respond to such "high service" levels while others told their friends and family members.

Soon the word spread about my excellent customer service. Customers would wait in line for me to assist them, even when other associates were available. "I'm here to see Mr. Hill," they would say. Customers would call the store before leaving their home asking if I was working. My Managerial role included several other responsibilities. I often stayed after my shift to complete everything. The extra work didn't bother me. Going out of my way to show kindness towards others helped heal the pain in my heart.

Carrying the hurt of my marriage and the disappointment associated with work weighed me down. It felt like I was in a wash and spin cycle of pain from my failing marriage and struggling career. But taking the focus off myself and showing kindness to others helped ease the pain and break the cycle. I never imagined that something as simple as kindness would be so powerful. "That is the nicest thing I've heard all day" was a response I heard often. Customers shared about loved ones dying and babies being born; I received letters and cards thanking me, all because I made them the focus and showed kindness during their visit. A simple way to keep myself out of the center of focus was remembering to have **J.O.Y. ... Jesus first, Others second, Yourself last.**

HIS SOLUTIONS

"Most important of all, continue to show deep love for each other, for love covers a multitude of sins." — *1 Peter 4:8 NLT*

LEVEL 5

HIS LOVE VS. MY FEAR (PART 1)

When God told me to base my life on love and kindness I did not realize that it would change everything in me. The first step was realizing how much God loved me. I remembered the scripture that said, "God is love" and that we should love one another. But somehow, I had looked at these verses from a religious point of view. I had not fully received that God loved me unconditionally. I guess my interpretation of this scripture was God liked me, and when I did good things, He liked me even more.

I began to confess that God loves me with the same love that He loves Jesus. It felt strange at first to say something so bold. The truth of the matter is that God so loved the world that he gave His Son, Jesus; so that he could deliver us from destruction. If he did not value us to an equivalent degree, He would not have made the exchange. I had to get beyond the knowledge in my head to believe in my heart that God loved me. Here is the verse that sealed this truth in my heart and not just my head.

> *"We have come to know and believe the love that God has for us. God is love, and whoever abides in love abides in God, and God abides in him.* — I John 4:16

When I began to meditate on these truths, I could feel my inner man being energized. I was accepting and internalizing the truth of

God's love for me. Knowing He loved me, despite my condition and my issues, gave me the strength to show love to others. Being convinced that God loved me despite my shortcomings gave me the perspective and more endurance to show love regardless of what was happening or how others responded.

As I would wake up extra early to spend time reading and meditating on God's Word – the Bible, I knew my workday was going to go well. This scripture freed me from the dread of going to work worried about the negative things that could happen and helped me to overcome my old attitude of selfish thinking when people and circumstances would try to get under my skin.

When I showed people love and kindness based only on the knowledge that it was a good thing to do, it was not lasting. I was tempted to revert back to my old attitude and selfish thinking when situations and circumstances would get under my skin.

> *"… we rejoice in our sufferings, knowing that suffering produces endurance, and endurance produces character, and character produces hope, and hope does not put us to shame, because God's love has been poured into our hearts through the Holy Spirit who has been given to us."* — Romans 5:3-5

Walking in Love as an Assistant Manager

Work was beginning to have a different feel for me now. One of my fellow Managers asked me, "What are you so excited and positive about these days?" I gave him an example that I had read about choosing your attitude. In the story, two prisoners were serving extended sentences. Their cells were made of cement walls and steel bars. While one man spent countless hours staring at the walls and bars, the other man spent his time remembering the stars in the night sky. The stars were not visible with his natural eye, but he imagined how they looked based on his previous experience. I told my coworker, we may be stuck in this store right now, but I have a vision of something better. He looked at me strangely and said, "No matter what you envision, you are still here at Cascade. "

Choosing to operate in love and joy propelled my confidence. I was less focused on being promoted, but instead I focused on how I could help someone else. Being promoted seemed almost impossible at that point of my career but showing love to others was a goal that I could achieve each day. It did not matter who the person was or what they needed; I put myself in a position to serve. While I focused on serving others, God began to restore my life. While I was still enduring the destruction of my marriage, God sent me an opportunity to serve.

Senior Management selected the Cascade store to host a new Management Trainee. Perry Smith had an MBA and a background in engineering. As a trainee his task was to learn how our stores operated. Upon successful completion of his program, he would become a part of the company's leadership team. Ideally, the store manager would allow the trainee to shadow him and provide the training as they went. But my Store Manager told Perry, "I want you to get with Kenny. He has been here a long time and he knows everything."

I was not sure if that was a vote of confidence for my ability to train people or if He did not feel like being bothered. Nevertheless, I was used to training people. I had prepared several others who were promoted to other positions. This time I did not mind.

The training got off to a great start for me. Perry Smith was also a trained pastor; he had been divorced before and remarried. Our sessions became more of him helping me, than me preparing him. It was good for me to be able to talk with someone who understood what I was facing. He provided encouragement and an example of what life could look like after divorce. Perry was also an expert in finances. He reviewed financial statements like a CEO. Spending time with him elevated my understanding of our company's financial reports dramatically. This relationship was a Godsend. I showed him everything I knew about The Home Depot, and he was sharing his life and encouraging me. He invited me to attend his church one Sunday, and I met his wife. To my surprise, his wife and I knew each other from college in San Diego. He and his wife were expecting their first child. They had such a loving environment around them that I wanted to be a part of it. I would stop by for dinner on weekends and when I did not want to be alone at my house, I would spend the night on their couch.

Watching Perry and his family gave me hope that my situation would change and that I, too, would have a loving family. Their home became a refuge for me. By the time Perry completed his training at my store location, he was ready to advance in his program. We had become good friends, and his wife introduced me to a friend of hers. This friend would eventually become my wife. By embracing what I could do for someone else, I received a friend for life and my wife. Without my new perspective on love and serving others, I might have avoided training someone else. Instead, God was able to bless my life in a way I could not have imagined.

Another opportunity to serve presented itself when a member of the store operations team came to our store. He was working on a pilot project to computerize some of the daily processes in the store. As the Assistant Manager for Operations, it made sense that I would have something to add to the discussion; however, the Store Manager asked me to help out in this project, instead of him. My daily routine required that I check in with several areas of the store to follow up. Nevertheless, I made myself available for as long as he needed. Once I saw his goal, I had some ideas to assist him with the process and the end-user functionality. We had a good work session with me explaining the difficulties we faced at the store level and him explaining how the project should ease some pain points. He was very appreciative of my time. I told him if I could be of any further assistance to call, and I welcomed him to come back to the store anytime he liked.

A few days later, he returned with some additional members of his team. I helped them and showed them some of the things we had discussed during our first visit. The information I shared seemed to be helpful to the entire team. I didn't realize it at the time, but the person responsible for this project was a Vice President who reported directly to the CEO of the company. He sent his team leader to my store because other project teams were overrunning the Cumberland store.

The Cumberland store was right across the highway from the Store Support Center (Corporate Office). The Store Support Center used the Cumberland store to test any new product or project the company was developing. The warm reception that I gave the team got back to the Vice President. A few days later, I received a call. It was the project team leader calling to ask me if I played basketball. "I used to play a lot, but not much lately," I replied. He invited me to a pick-up game the next morning at 5:30 am. I had the urge to say thanks but no thanks when he said, "Just come out; you'll be glad you did." I responded, "OK, I will."

I usually woke up early each morning to pray. This morning I did most of my praying on the way to the gym. When I arrived, I was relieved to see cars in the parking lot. I wasn't the only one there at 5:15 in the morning. Once the door opened, everyone went inside and started stretching, so I did the same. I found the project team leader and told him thank you for the invite. He grabbed me and said, "Hey Ken, let me introduce you to someone." At that moment, I was walked over to his boss, the Vice President of Operations where he said. "Ken, this is Brian." At this point, Brian said, "Nice to meet you, and thanks for helping with the project."

Just then, two people that I recognized walked to the free-throw line to shoot to see who got first pick for their team. I was shocked. I saw the Second and Third highest-ranking Officers in The Home Depot. I was overcome. I was invited to play basketball with almost the entire Executive Leadership Team of the company. By the end of the second week of playing, I knocked the rust off of my basketball game and was on a first-name basis with everyone. We met and played ball for a year until the gym had to have the floors refinished. After that, the group split up into a few different locations that were even further away.

During that year, I met people and made connections, and received mentoring that benefited my career exponentially.

I couldn't have navigated my way into that circle of leaders if I tried for years. It was God's favor opening the door and my heart to serve others providing the path. God showed me that if I stayed focused on His mission of offering Christ-like leadership to my associates, He would give me the exposure and connections that I needed. Later the following year, I was promoted from Assistant Manager at the Cascade store to the Cumberland store as a Co-Store Manager. The Cumberland store was so busy with its sales volume and company pilots that they utilized a second Store Manager position to keep the store on track.

I worked at the Cascade store as an Assistant Manager for six years. The first four years were full of toil and difficulty. After my marriage crumbled and I embraced the call to love, it took two short years for me to be promoted. During this two-year period, I devoted myself to serving on my job and at my church. I gave freely of my time and finances to support the gospel. The teachings I had received were a vital part of my recovery.

LEVEL 6

His Love vs. My Fear (Part 2)

A s I prepared to transition to my new role, I was keenly aware that love had paved the way for this unique opportunity. The passion shown towards my associates and Customers had elevated my impact as a leader. Love displayed through kindness towards vendors, suppliers, and the community had made me the person to contact at the Cascade store. Love and compassion had created a personal brand that I would have never been able to develop on my own. It was a lifestyle that uplifted me and those around me instead of the artificial image that ran people away from me.

For each level of relationship, I decided to show love. Fear and selfishness were always bidding for my attention. I chose to respond in patience through love, not anger through fear when things appeared to go wrong with associates or customers. Staying calm because I trusted in God's provision for the situation allowed me to focus on what He was directing me to do.

Walking in Love as a Store Manager

On one occasion I was helping a contractor load his purchase of 80lb. bags of concrete. We loaded a few, and then I asked to sign off on his receipt. The receipt showed that he paid for five bags. After putting the fifth bag in his truck, I thanked him for shopping with us. He looked bewildered and said, "No, I told the cashier that I needed ten bags for this job." I apologized for the cashier charging him for the wrong amount and told him that I would load them into his truck if he paid for the five additional bags. The customer went inside, and I waited. After five minutes, he had not returned, so I went inside to see what happened. I asked the cashier where the customer was. She said he went to the Customer Service Desk. I called the Customer Service Desk to ask what was going on. The Associate told me that the customer didn't have any more money and was using our phone to call his customer to pay for the additional concrete bags.

This customer had planned to help himself to five additional bags of concrete without paying for them. My first thought was how much inventory and money we lost each year to people like this. Tens of thousands of dollars would show up missing during inventory due to this type of theft. I had several ways to respond to the situation.

None of my associates knew that he had tried to take the additional bags. There were a couple of options that I could have used to show the gentleman that this type of business was not welcomed. I could have called the on-duty police officer to threaten him with attempted thief. I could tell him to come back when he got the money, and I would be glad to help load him. Instead, the scripture inside of my apron popped into my mind.

> "*Love bears up under anything, and everything that comes, and is ever ready to believe the best of every person.*"
> — 1 Corinthians 13:7

I began thinking the best about this customer who was trying to steal from my store. As I walked towards the Customer Service Desk, my thoughts were focused on how I could show kindness, not the fear of loss to the customer. When I arrived, the customer was still on the phone trying in vain to reach his customer. I pulled out my credit card and told the Associate to ring up five concrete bags. I walked back out to his truck and loaded up the concrete. When I went back inside, I didn't see the customer. The Customer Service Associate called me and told me that the customer was amazed that I paid for the concrete. He went on to ask them to say, "Thank You" and that he would never shop anywhere else. The customer became a faithful supporter of the store for many years. He was converted from someone who shopped occasionally and pilfered from us to a committed customer by one act of kindness.

Opportunities to respond in love versus reacting in fear were all around me. In each instance, I learned to resist fear and lean into love. Becoming entrenched in love also helped me readily identify when others were using fear-based tactics; even if it was my boss, a peer, or one of my associates. At times, I found myself filtering fear driven messages from a Senior Leader and delivering it to my team from a love-based perspective.

The point of focus was typically around accountability for some metric or process, including managing markdowns, payroll hours, or sales performance. Reminding my team that we were responsible for the relationships with our customers, partners, vendors, and shareholders was my priority. I encouraged my team that these relationships are centered on trust and commitment. Execution required the associates to execute our operational plan at a consistently high level. I found that getting associates to remember and focus on our commitment was the first step. I would then follow up to see if they needed help getting it done. Staying focused on the dynamic of trust worked more successfully than switching back and forth between incentives and reprimands.

Walking in Love as District Manager

In Ephesians 3:20 we are reminded that God is able to do exceedingly, abundantly above all that we can ask or imagine. Being promoted to the role of District Manager was more than I had hoped. As a Store Manager my focus had been on my associates, customers, and the community for over five years. When I was named a possible candidate for promotion to District Manager, I was surprised.

My marriage and our first daughter being born meant that staying in Atlanta was the best family decision. I determined to do what was best for my family, even if it meant passing on a promotion. After all that God had done in bringing my wife and I together, I would not allow career aspirations to strain our marriage.

Being promoted from Store manager to District Manager would be a life-changing event. Even more, to become a District Manager in Atlanta where the company was founded, and still operates its headquarters was a dream. Management carefully and critically examined the most experienced and successful District Managers for the Atlanta market positions. Store Managers in Atlanta were usually promoted to districts in a different area of the country to learn their new role and become established.

Many believe that the District Manager role is the best position in the company. As a District Manager, you are entrusted to establish a business culture and deliver results across ten stores. Some District Managers advanced in the company to roles on the senior leadership team. Others managed to consistently produce talent for the company and trustworthy metrics as well. As a solid performing District Manager, one would have input on company-wide projects. You could develop established relationships with the organization's top brass but also stay connected with the associates and Customers. The caveat to these benefits was delivering consistent performance across your team. Achieving consistent, sustainable results from ten or more stores required genuine leadership.

I watched different District Managers and their leadership styles. Some of them lead through fear and intimidation. Everyone's good standing or career was always seemingly on the line. When this type of leader visited a store, the associates ran away from them. Everybody tried to become as busy as possible, doing anything to keep them from being confronted. The store's management team could not hide, even if they wanted to. They had to step up and face criticism for whatever was not right in the building. This type of leader excelled in finding something wrong and letting you know they saw it and gave an occasional compliment along with a list of things to be completed.

This fear-based leadership expressed through anger caused the store team to react and find quick fixes that usually were not sustainable. When the District Manager showed anger or displeasure during a visit, the associates knew that the Store Manager would be upset after the visit was over. Everyone tried to avoid the Store Manager after a visit from his/her boss. This type of store visit would drain the team's energy and enthusiasm, which the Store Manager worked to build. Finally, fear-based administration raised the stress level for everyone, including the District Manager. I witnessed many healthy, vibrant people become unhappy and unhealthy leaders. Unhealthy stress levels and unrealistic work schedules compromised people who remained attached to this leadership style.

It was good that I learned early in my career that performance effort did not always translate to success. My trust had to be in God and not my ability to make people do what was needed. The hard lesson that I learned early in my career was a valuable one. I was seeing the evidence in the lives of others and felt compassion for them. So many of them could never bring themselves to trust in anything but themselves. Trusting in your strength or the strength of others sets you up for failure and defeat. The senior leadership of the company saw this trend and began to address it. They had measures to address unhealthy behaviors, but years of fear-based performance did not stop immediately. I determined that I would not become this type of leader.

"Cursed is the man that trusts in man and makes flesh his strength, whose heart turns away from the Lord." — *Jeremiah 17:5*

There was a rigorous process of interviews and assessments designed to identify the best District Manager candidates from all over the company. Time and time again, God's wisdom and favor showed up for me. I once encountered a leader who doubted my ability and readiness for the role. He scheduled me to meet him at a different store for a business review. I knew a good District Manager should be able to walk into any store, review the store's metrics, evaluate strengths, and opportunities of the business. The next step would be to ask the right questions for the store team to gain understanding of the root causes and behaviors. If this were done correctly, the associates and management team would be able to provide recommendations for the adjustments needed. I was nervous about the meeting because his decision would play a significant role in me moving forward to the next stage of the evaluation process.

Through the financial training I received from Perry Smith and God's wisdom during the meeting, I provided responses that caused the Vice President leading the review to say, "I learned something new from our time today." One by one, God turned my critics into supporters. I could not do it alone. For every District Manager position that opened, there were several available candidates to fill it. Some of these candidates had earned support from the highest levels of leadership in the company. It was the favor of God in my life and His purpose that made the difference.

I remember when the phone call came offering me the promotion. I was celebrating with my store team at our annual Christmas party. My cell phone rang, and I saw it was the Vice President calling. I stepped away to take the call and listened as my life was elevated to another level. I was not only receiving an upgraded compensation package; my area of influence and access were now changing. One thing that I had determined not to change was my focus on love.

My approach to building a team and getting exceptional results at Cascade made me a candidate for the District Manager role. It was God's grace and favor showing up for me. God orchestrated everything in just the right timing for promotion to the district closest to my home.

Unfortunately, when I was a promoted as District Manager, I caved into the pressure to hold people accountable due to pressure from fear-driven leaders. Instead of following my established process, I reacted in fear and documented people on my team for missing established metrics. I was not outside of company policy for doing this, but it went against my message and operating method. When I bounced back and forth between love and fear it diluted the message and confused my team. It was a perfect opportunity to reaffirm the patience principle and increase the trust level with my team. Instead, I gave in to the need to show that I was holding people accountable. I moved away from what had worked for me for years as a Store Manager.

As a new District Manager my actions were scrutinized more heavily. People watched how I handled my team. I had a perfect process and a proven track record, but I laid it down. I was more concerned that Senior Leadership would view my process unfavorably. I gave in to and reacted to fear. Allowing fear to enter damaged the trust that I was establishing with my team and was a mistake. I wish I would have stood my ground, trusting God as I had so many times before.

> *"Fearing people is a dangerous trap, but trusting the Lord means safety." — Proverbs 29:25*

Through this situation it was reinforced that fear reacts, but love responds. I had been through these scenarios before. Why would I resort to reacting in fear after I had been firmly established in love and trust? I allowed the enemy to make me think that there was too much on the line, specifically my reputation. Fear makes you focus on yourself, and selfishness gives fear its power. I allowed the enemy to get me thinking about self-preservation instead of looking to the interest of others. I had learned this lesson years ago during my divorce, but the enemy looks for any opportunity to plant fear into our lives. This was a learning opportunity for me and a reminder to remain committed to love and trust.

When I arrived at one of my stores, I wanted people to run towards me and not away from me. I sought to make sure to notice and recognize associates for even the smallest detail or evidence of upholding our values. I wanted them to show me what they were working on and what they were proud of doing. I wanted to know if something I was expecting was not realistic and why. So, I focused on the people, especially those who were not easy to see. One of my routines for each store was to go back into the shipping and receiving or outside in the garden area. I would spend time working with these employees for hours. Bringing my lunch and eating in the break room was a surprise to the associates and a great way to connect with them, also.

Connecting with the associates allowed me to respond in love. By listening to what they wanted to talk about, I learned how to improve things for them. By sitting and eating in the break room, I got a chance to see if having one refrigerator was enough to fit everyone's lunch or if another one was needed. Focusing on the details of what was best for them was a way to express and highlight love instead of fear. Going beyond the associates' expectations caused them to go beyond the customers' expectations.

This focus caused my stores to respond tremendously. After a short time, my team began to lead the region in significant performance areas. I was receiving performance awards and recognition beyond my dreams. My focus on love for so many years had built strong relationships that endured. Associates and customers alike would assist with anything that I was doing. My team excelled during great economic times as well as during downturns. My decision to lead through love instead of fear was the best business decision I could have made. This decision also lifted me from personal despair. I was placed on a course to exceed my career goals and achieve a marriage based on serving one another.

LEVEL 7

His Restoration

The Bible story of Joseph is full of many life lessons. The depth of his trials and the height of his triumph is remarkable. One thing that caught my attention about Joseph's experience is this truth.

> *Until the time came to fulfill his dreams, the Lord tested Joseph's character. — Psalm 105:19*

The Lord tested Joseph's character with many trials before He fulfilled his dream and brought restoration. I imagine the most challenging time he experienced was the two years he waited after interpreting the King's Cup Bearer and Baker's dreams. Joseph foretold that the cupbearer would be restored to his position. The cupbearer had to be thrilled with Joseph's prediction. When it came true, three days later, Joseph asked the cupbearer to remember him. Joseph had to have high expectations that his situation would soon change. The Bible records that it was a full two years later that Joseph stood before the King.

One's character gets tested over and over again. Consistently doing the right thing and doing it the right way when no one is paying attention is the character that is needed. I was challenged to develop my character, however, like Joseph, God richly rewarded me in time. One day the District Human Resource Manager stopped by the store. Most of that visit they spent in the training room working on their laptop.

They talked with a few associates, and a few minutes later, they left the store. A short time later, I stopped by the training room and noticed a report lying on the table where they had been working. I picked up the information and hurried to see if I could catch them. By the time I reached the parking lot, it was too late; they were gone. I looked at the report to see what it was. I was holding a confidential salary printout for all the Assistant Managers in the District. This report had every Manager ranked by percentile from the highest paid to the lowest. I looked for my name and found it. I was in the bottom five percent based on salary.

The enemy went right to work telling me how crazy I was to pay tithes and give at my church. The enemy attacked with "Look at where you are financially. And you still give. You are barely living from paycheck to paycheck. No wonder your wife left you; you're not practical. You work at the most difficult store. You have more education and experience than 90 percent of these people, and you're at the bottom of this list." I felt like I had the air knocked out of me. But I tried to remind myself, "This is not about me. Choose to focus on others."

This episode challenged my character for the next few years. I continued to train people who were well above my salary. I had to maintain focus on doing my best work even while being underpaid. There was no quick fix to this situation. Allocated raises were largely based on the store's performance and my store had a long way to go before my performance level could demand the adjustment I needed.

The areas of the business that I inherited were under constant scrutiny. I oversaw the Operational Departments of the store. This department represented the largest group of associates in the building. My areas of responsibility included the Cashiers, the Customer Service Desk, the Receiving Department, the Return to Vendor Department, the Computer Room, and Cash Vault area. Getting each location to perform consistently was a tremendous task. I had been warned that if things did not turn around soon, I would lose my job.

One day the Store Manager and his boss (District Manager) called me into the Office. They had just received the results of an unannounced audit of my departments. The frustrated look on their faces told me that they did not find enough evidence to terminate me. I had been working extremely hard to get my team to follow procedures consistently.

The audit found positive progress in almost every area. I breathed a sigh of relief just before the District Manager slammed the paperwork on the desk. My boss then threatened, "The next time any of your areas are not up to standard, it will take God Himself to save your job."

Wow, he knew I was a Christian, so I guess he added the God reference for added effect. Now, I was the lowest paid Manager and soon to be unemployed if my boss had his way.

I told God this wasn't fair, but it would not stop me from doing what I was supposed to do. I had no idea what God had in store for me. My hope was for things to change in my finances, career, and marriage. I needed a life change. I was determined to keep giving, serving others, and responding in love. I had invested too much to quit. I was being rebuilt by love and couldn't risk taking my focus away from it. As painful as this news was, I had to push forward, keep going until I experienced God's faithfulness for myself.

Joseph spent thirteen years in Egypt before his deliverance. He spent the last two years waiting for a response to his gifting. A time and season came that made him essential to the Kingdom. The Cupbearer remembered him. Joseph was brought before Pharaoh and elevated to Prime Minister of Egypt. Joseph had passed the test, and God repaid him for all his trials. In every area that Joseph suffered pain, confusion, or grief; God restored him. His brothers had stripped away the coat his father had given him, but now Joseph received an elegant linen wardrobe with a gold chain and the King's signet ring. His brothers had despised him, but now Joseph was given authority over the entire land of Egypt. Joseph married and had two sons. He named the first Manasseh, which means God has made me forget all my toil and father's family. His second son was called Ephraim, which means God has made me fruitful in the land of my grief.

I often thought of Joseph's story and how God vindicated him. During my struggles, I wondered if God would similarly transform my life. God seemed to keep track of everything Joseph endured and rewarded him in every area that he had suffered. The family members who mocked and ridiculed him for his dreams came bowing down to him. Despite their harsh treatment towards him, Joseph forgave them because he saw that God was directing his path. Joseph entered Egypt as a slave, was put into prison but rose to the palace. If God did it for Joseph, there was hope for me. My life was in a financial and relational pit. I had to believe that God was taking notice and keeping track of my tears and suffering.

Several years passed, but God remembered the salary report and the threat to fire me. It seemed that God kept a detailed checklist of the hurt and pain in my life. The same way God recompensed Joseph for the hurt in his life, God did the same for me. Just like Joseph, I had to persevere during the process, but God came through with His checklist of promises for my life.

Several years passed since I found the salary list with my name at the bottom. God had transformed my life in every area. I remarried a woman who loved and appreciated me. We were celebrating our first daughter's birth, and my career was rising beyond anything I could imagine. I was a District Manager with the top-performing team in the region. I was receiving all types of awards and recognition for excellent performance. Also, I appeared on the Steve Harvey radio and television shows. The company awarded me an all-expense-paid trip for two to a five-star Caribbean Resort. My wife and I were at such peace with one another and began looking for our dream house.

One day, I received a letter from the company's compensation department. The letter was a 401K contribution adjustment notice. Since my compensation was now in the top 5% of the company, I was given notice that I would have to reduce my contribution level. Wow, this is amazing, I thought. Just then, I heard the spirit of God whisper, "I'm paying you back. You didn't quit, and I didn't forget." I had to think for a moment, then it hit me, the salary report! That's when I felt like God said, "Yes, the report presented the bad news on paper, so I made sure the good news came on paper." I had forgotten entirely about the salary report. I quickly recalled the pain and despair I had felt but I lifted my hands and said, "You are so Faithful, God!" He rescued me from that financial pit.

Furthermore, He caused me to forget about the pain and suffering I had endured. My life had become so full of joy, love, and generosity that I had completely forgotten about it. It was almost like it happened to someone else and that I only heard about it. At this moment, I could relate to what Joseph experienced in the naming of his sons. God had also made me forget my years of toil and had made me fruitful in the land of my grief.

Months later, I received a phone call. It was from my former boss, the Store Manager who threatened to fire me. He left the company several years earlier to work for a different company. Things had not gone as planned, and he wanted to return to The Home Depot. He was calling me to ask to interview for an Assistant Manager job in one of my stores. I could hear the desperation in his voice, and I knew that he had been out of work for some time. I remembered Joseph and his brothers. Joseph realized that it was God who directed his path to Egypt. He did not hold it against his brothers for selling him into slavery. In Genesis 50:20, Joseph told his brothers," You intended to harm me, but God intended it for good, to accomplish what is now being done, the saving of many lives." I was now in a position to assist my former boss in gaining employment and helping his household. I told him that I would be glad to set up an interview and looked forward to what he could add to my team. He was hired as an Assistant Manager a short time afterward. I never asked him about his threatening to fire me. I treated him with honor and respect as a valued leader on my team. Getting even or retribution never crossed my mind. I knew that my character had changed. I was operating in love like my Father's nature.

I thought about the many lives that were spared because Joseph endured the process and maintained his character. The famine was worldwide, and without Joseph's God given wisdom and execution of God's plan, millions of lives could have been lost to starvation. In my experience, God used me to encourage support and pray for many of my associates.

I had two of my associates share that they were contemplating suicide when they crossed my path. God used me in both of those situations to listen, encourage, and pray for them. One of these people came to me while they were struggling with suicidal thoughts and needed counseling. I saw the second person at a wedding of a mutual friend. We had not seen each other for several years. They shared that because I hired them, they changed their mind about committing suicide. Because I believed in them enough to hire them, they wanted to keep their word and show up to work. By merely being where I was purposed to be and enduring, God's promises came to fruition and lives were saved.

Joseph went into Egypt with talent and gifts. Through his trials, he developed the character needed for the destiny God had in store for him. It's often during the most challenging situations in our lives that character develops the most. My path from toil to blessing was not by chance. I may have prolonged the time of my toiling, but once I surrendered; God was there. He was willing and ready to help me develop my character. As God transformed me to align with his nature (love), I experienced a change. It was a change on the inside that transformed my external condition. More than a raise, not just a promotion, or a better marriage relationship; I experienced something deeper. I experienced a total transformation of identity, nature, and priorities.

Joseph's time of preparation was for a season when he would become essential for Egypt's kingdom and the entire world. His character and gifting were instrumental on a worldwide scale. Likewise, I believe a season is coming where people of character, people developed in God's nature, will be essential to the Kingdom of God. I believe this is why God has you reading this book for "such a time as this."

Success in the assignment that God has for our lives is not based on talent but character. We are tested in the areas of our character that are crucial to the completion of our assignment. Passing the character test shows that we can be trusted with the position, authority, and resources that God will entrust us with. I can assure you that your season of preparation will probably look a lot different than you expect.

LEVEL 8

HIS INVITATION

Developing the heart of a servant leader was game changing for my career. Genuine servant leadership focuses on the best interest of others with no desire or expectation of personal gain. Servant leaders are comfortable serving when there is no perceived benefit. It is about serving when there is no audience to applaud you and no recognition to be received. This type of serving comes from the heart. It requires a deep desire to benefit those you are serving. Servant leaders trust God to compensate in the way and the season that He chooses.

The level of trust and engagement that I developed with my associates and customers played a role in my moving from Assistant Manager to Co-Store Manager. I became focused on how I could help my associates set and reach personal goals. In the back of my mind, the underlying purpose was still to improve the business. It was not the same self-centered desire for a promotion that I was driven by early in my career, but it was still the expected result.

My tenure at the Cumberland store was approaching one year when my District Manager asked me if I would go back and run the Cascade store, temporarily. The Store Manager had unexpectedly left the company for another opportunity. The District Manager assumed that I was not interested in going back to Cascade permanently. However, he needed me to run the store for a month while he identified the right candidate. I told him his assumption was correct, but I was willing to help even though I was in a suitable place at Cumberland.

The thought of leaving the Cumberland store with all of its bells and whistles to return to Cascade was not appealing. The distance between the stores was only 12 miles. But the difference in the experience was like night and day. Cumberland was almost one and a half times the size of Cascade in square footage and employed twice the number of associates. In one year, I had experienced a completely different view of the company. During a regular workday, I interacted with leaders from every area of the organization. I even developed relationships with the CEO and his family. We hosted visits from the company's Board of Directors and a Cabinet Member of the President of the United States. It was a dream job. This type of exposure did not happen anywhere else in the company.

The expectations and standards were high. We worked long hard hours, but they were hours of excitement and anticipation. As a leadership team we were developing associates and seeing them get promoted to Supervisor roles. Several Supervisors advanced to Assistant Manager positions and one of our Assistant Managers was elevated to become a Store Manager. The Corporate Office recruited several of our associates to fill roles. All of this happened in less than a year. The store was meeting or exceeding all financial and operational metrics, and we were training and developing people. These were the traits of a highly effective leadership team. The District Manager and Vice President recognized my contribution to the store's turnaround, and my future looked brighter than ever. I looked forward to returning from my short visit to Cascade as soon as a new Store Manager was selected.

A high level of excitement from the associates and some customers met my return to Cascade. Yet, it did not take me long to see that the store had fallen on hard times. It had been a year since the CEO visit, my promotion, and the store experiencing some success. There had been optimism for the positive trend to continue. Instead, I arrived to find low customer service scores, the store missing sales plan, and the associate morale sinking. It seemed that a lot of the momentum that was in place a year earlier had dissipated, entirely. The celebration welcoming me back lasted for about a week. After which, people went back to their normal behavior. The associates ignored both the customers and the business standards. I told myself, "I'm only here for a month while they find a new Store Manager." As soon as I finished that thought, it hit me. This mindset was the attitude that so many of the previous store leaders had about the store. Even worse, I had experienced years of that leadership mindset, and now I was thinking the same way. I could pass the time and I would soon be back at the Cumberland store with all the comfort and advantages that I had left.

Then, I was reminded of what I had dreamed of seeing happen for the Cascade associates and customers. I remembered how I wanted the associates to experience advancement in their careers. It was at this point that I asked myself, "Am I going to leave the palace at Cumberland to go back to the pit where I had previously spent six years? At first, it did not make sense. I kept asking myself why I would, after having survived and finally been promoted from Cascade, now subject myself and my career a second time to go back to Cascade. There was no guarantee that things were going to change or improve. I could simply choose to return to all the benefits of the Cumberland store, building my brand and increasing my exposure to new opportunities. However, the vision of seeing the team at Cascade achieve at the highest level was still burning inside me. It had not died.

Deep inside I always wanted the store associates to receive the recognition and opportunities for promotion that had eluded them. I wanted the customers to experience consistent service levels that they only caught a glimpse of before I was promoted.

For years, my desire had been for my promotion and increase. When I engaged with God in my time of need, He put new desires in me. I now desired to see others improve and advance their careers, and for the community to experience true partnership from its local store. These desires were now speaking louder than the path to higher recognition and comfort. Again, it was God drawing me to mission and purpose. I was still assigned to be a leader dedicated to these associates, showing them Christ-centered leadership. I was supposed to help them make the changes necessary to experience success in their lives and careers. He was inviting me to co-labor with Him in serving the associates and customers of the Cascade store.

> "Delight yourself in the Lord, and He will give you the desires of your heart." — Psalm 37:4

It had been a while since I had thought about the mission and focus that He had given me seven years earlier. I began to struggle with going back to Cumberland or staying to complete the task. It was then that something extraordinary happened. I remembered how God had completely removed the burdens, pain, and sorrow of my marriage, finances, and career. He had completely restored my finances. I had met and was dating my future wife. The heaviness and anxiety about my future that used to permeate my thoughts were gone. All of these had been a heavy burden to carry. Through love and kindness, the burden had been removed from my life and destroyed. During my temporary assignment, God placed a new burden on me. God showed me the team of associates at the Cascade store. He showed me how they had little to no hope and were full of anxiety about their futures. This new burden was compassion for the store team. I developed a great sense of compassion and empathy for them. I had experienced their frustration and had been in a similar state. A consuming desire to see the situations in their lives change overcame me. I experienced something similar to the compassion Jesus was moved with when He fed the five thousand.

> "And Jesus when he came out, He saw a great multitude of people and was moved with compassion for them, because they were like sheep not having a shepherd. So, he began to teach them many things." — Mark 6:34

The store team needed and deserved a leader committed to serve and teach them to succeed. God was asking me to accept the mission He had given me. I would not be doing it alone; He was inviting me to co-labor with Him.

During the last few days before I was scheduled to return to Cumberland, this burden became almost unbearable. There had not been a promotion from the Cascade store in over ten years except for mine. The associates worked for a great company but were not receiving the best it had to offer. I called the District Manager and told him that I wanted to take the store permanently and turn it around.

Aligned with His Assignment

I was nervous, but I knew that I was doing what God wanted me to do. As I look back on that decision it was the best career decision I ever made. Through my compassion for the success of the associates, God taught me servant leadership. I began spending time and investing in the team because I was hungry for them to experience a change. I was not expecting anything for myself, but I had to get them to share what I had helped create at Cumberland. They deserved to enjoy the full benefits of working for one of the best companies in the world.

Teaching the team what I had learned would not be a quick or easy process. Transformation didn't happen overnight in my life. This change is a process. There were times it appeared that nobody was receiving what I was instructing them to do. I was reminded that it was my job to model and instruct the principles and that God would cause it to sink into their hearts. Being consistent in my role helped to keep the standard in front of them. God was working and causing people to see things differently and ultimately respond differently. This process was teaching me patience. Remaining consistent in my level of service to the team regardless of circumstances accomplished what words alone could never do. I was extending this same level of service and patience towards customers, vendors, and partners on any level.

One day, I received a request to assist the Marketing Department by building a display. Instead of simply assigning the request over to one of my Assistant Managers to fulfill, I took the time to listen and find out exactly what the details were. It turned out that Melissa Saunders was a Senior Marketing Manager for The Home Depot. Melissa was responsible for all multicultural marketing and was working on a collaboration for one of Tom Joyner's Fantastic Voyage Cruises. Tom Joyner was an early member of the Commodores Band with Lionel Richie. Tom became a pioneer in morning and afternoon radio broadcasting. He was known as the hardest working man in radio. Mr. Joyner hosted Caribbean cruises that were packed with faithful listeners from all over the country. The Home Depot was sponsoring a "How to Install a Faucet" workshop on one of the cruises. When the request came in, I didn't know who or what the display was for. I was simply asked if I could build a faucet installation display that was clear or see through. I took personal interest in finding out the specifics of how it would be used and who would be using it. Through my focus on delivering the best solution for the project, I learned who Melissa was and the details of the event.

I took special interest in this project being successful for Melissa and her team. I enlisted one of my associates who was an artist to build the display. Michael Scofield was a stickler for details so I knew that his solution would exceed expectations. The display worked perfectly, and the event was a success.

This connection paved the way for me to be considered for the Steve Harvey show years later. I wasn't expecting anything. I was only helping make someone else's project successful. I challenged myself daily to be a blessing to everyone who crossed my path. There were times that the results of meeting that goal were immediately seen in the smiles and "thank you's" that I received. There were times when nothing significant appeared to happen at first but over time the impact was seen. Serving others earnestly and expecting nothing in return began to build a brand for me and my store. I challenged my team to consistently extend themselves and go out of their way on behalf of our customers and others.

This mindset began to galvanize my team around customer service. The metrics for customer service had been a struggle for the store for as long as the metric had been tracked. Slowly and steadily, our performance scores started to change. I challenged my team with becoming the best customer service environment in the city. My team responded and rose to the top of the customer service rankings for the first time. We still had a long way to go in terms of store appearance and several other areas, but we had the right focus. It wasn't long before we were at the top of all performance metrics across the board. Achieving and sustaining top tier performance in a highly competitive environment is not an easy task. Accomplishing this level of success in a place that had never experienced it before required transformational leadership. God's transformation of my life provided the basis for the transformation of an entire store. The associates who watched me change responded to that change and to the call to be transformed in their mindsets. When I asked my team what they appreciated about my leadership the most consistent response was "You love people." Associates who came from other stores often said, "It's different here at Cascade, it's like a family."

When I think about the rewards and favor that I experienced in my career, most of it happened while I was the Store Manager at the Cascade store. The store's turnaround earned most of my leadership awards. My promotion to the District Manager role was based on what I accomplished as the Cascade Store Manager.

The most rewarding thing for me was seeing the associates experience promotion and advancement. God showed me that being in line with His mission for my life and career would cause His goodness to find me, even at Cascade. It was there that I accepted the invitation to co-labor with God to reach people with His love. I was reminded that God sent Jesus because we were in dire need, and He desperately wanted to show us His love. God continues to send His sons and daughters into places that are thirsting for His love when we accept His invitation to co-labor with Him.

CO-LABORING

*"So, Jesus explained, 'I tell you the truth, the Son can do nothing by himself. He does only what he sees the Father doing. Whatever the Father does, the Son also does." —
John 5:19 NLT*

LEVEL 9

PATHWAY TO POWER

---

ooking back on my career experiences and my transformation, I often wondered if the process could have evolved differently. Could I have totally surrendered my life and career to God and walked in love without the devastation that I experienced? I would like to say that I could have surrendered everything to him, however; I had the opportunity to and failed to do so. I was content with loving God and being nice to people, while my faith was kept for my personal use. Only when I desired something that required more income, or a promotion did my faith turn to God.

The question arises whether my suffering was necessary. Without the suffering and pain, would I have ever experienced the same levels of influence and success? Looking back, I am convinced that there would not have been the same level of success in my career and life. This conclusion is not based on my personal experience alone. I have come to understand that God allows us to see the faulty foundation we build upon. But like Joseph, it was necessary for the testing. God allows tests for the building of testimonies. Throughout history, many leaders serve as examples. I choose Jesus's example of enduring suffering. His suffering led to a greater connection to love, which produced power and influence that remains unmatched. In fact, He went through several levels of trial and opposition with each producing a level of power that propelled him towards His destiny.

In Mark 1:11, John the Baptist baptized Jesus in the Jordan river and God spoke from heaven and said, *"You are my beloved Son, in whom I am well pleased."* Then Jesus was led into the wilderness, where he fasted forty days. During this forty day fast, Jesus was tempted by the devil. The temptation centered around two topics. The devil tested Jesus's identity to see if Jesus knew who He was ("if thou be the son of God…"). Secondly, Jesus was presented with the opportunity to focus on Himself and take a short cut to fulfill His assignment ("All these things will I give thee if thou will bow down and worship me"). Jesus resisted and endured the temptations.

Identity and process are important concepts to have clarity in one's life. The devil still uses the same tricks to trip people up and drag them off course. Identity was the same attack he used against Adam and Eve in the garden of Eden. If you recall the serpent baited them with a question, "Has God said." Then the devil presented a lie mixed with a partial truth, "You shall not surely die." The devil then added "God does know that in the day you eat thereof you shall be like God knowing good and evil." This was a partial truth which equals a lie. Adam and Eve were already like God. God created them in His image and His likeness and wanted them to know only good. (See Gen1:26-27). The devil's lie worked because Adam and Eve thought God was holding something back from them. They thought they were taking a shortcut to become like God when they were already like Him. God created them to be the representation of God on the earth just like He was in heaven.

Since identity and a shortcut worked with Adam, the devil tried the same thing with Jesus. Satan's plan did not work because Jesus knew who he was. His Father had just reminded Him at His baptism *"This is my Beloved Son in whom I am well pleased."* Each time the devil tried to present partial truth; Jesus responded with the whole truth *"It is written."* Jesus understood the word of God intimately and could not be fooled.

Finally, the devil presented Jesus with a shortcut. Offering to give him all the kingdoms of the world for bowing down to him just once. Jesus knew His assignment involved suffering. He told His disciples several times. Jesus had full knowledge of the road before Him and the glory that would be His once the mission was completed. He chose to endure the suffering for our sake instead of bowing down to Satan. He focused on His Father's will and our benefit, not His own comfort.

> Jesus said, "… *the Son of Man must suffer many things and be rejected by the elders, the chief priests, and the teachers of the law, and he must be killed and on the third day raised to life.*" — Luke 9:22

As a result, Jesus operated in power, miracles, and fulfilled the law, providing the framework for the new covenant. The Bible in Luke 4 gives details of the power that accompanied Jesus after this time of suffering:

> "*He (Jesus) returned in the power of the Spirit into Galilee: and there went out a fame of him through all the region.*" — *Luke 4:14*

> "… *the people were astonished at His doctrine for His word was with power.* — *Luke 4:32*

> "…*the people were amazed and said "What a word is this! For with authority and power he commands the unclean spirits and they come out.*" — *Luke 4:36*

The Bible clearly tells us that Jesus has delegated power to His followers to overcome the devil.

Jesus said, *"... Behold I give unto you power to tread on serpents and scorpions, and all the power of the enemy and nothing shall by any means harm you. — Luke 10:19*

Jesus was affirmed in the love of the Father (This is my Beloved Son in whom I am well pleased). From there he successfully endured trials and then operated in power.

Jesus also endured suffering in the Garden of Gethsemane to the extent of sweating blood. Mark 14:34 records, Jesus said, "My soul is exceedingly sorrowful unto death." Jesus experienced mental anguish associated with being crucified. During this time, we see the love and trust relationship He had with His Father as He ends His prayer for relief with "not my will but Thy will be done."

Jesus received strength to endure being betrayed, arrested, falsely accused, whipped, and crucified. He willingly suffered all of this even though He possessed the power to obliterate His oppressors with a single word. Instead, Luke 23:34 records that He prayed *"Father, forgive them for they do not know what they are doing."* While innocent, Jesus allowed Himself to be crucified. He then descended into hell and took back the authority over death and the grave. He rose from the dead with all power in heaven, on earth and under the earth.

Empowered to Overcome

Not all suffering produces success nor does all pain result in power. Yet, Jesus' example of enduring suffering and pain was successful in accomplishing God's purposes. Suffering exists for many reasons. Primarily, suffering exists because we live in a fallen world. However, suffering may be self-inflicted like some of mine was. At other times, we can be assaulted by circumstances or tragedy.

The central matter of suffering is that when we turn to God in hard times, He is there. If we will receive God's love and develop our trust in Him, we become empowered to overcome. Not only will we be enabled to endure the turmoil of our condition, but we also become people of influence. God will empower us to go and shine His love light for others to see.

After believing God's love for me and walking in love towards others, I was entrusted with influence and authority. This influence and authority did not come from my job title or tenure with the company. I was still an Assistant Manager, however when I began to speak, people listened, and associates responded. Because I had invested in them, they were willing to exert discretionary effort for my cause. The same programs and initiatives that the store had previously failed to accomplish gradually started to work when I was in charge. The store ran differently when I was present. Things were done on time at a higher level of excellence. Associates who were notorious for being lackadaisical would pull their own weight during my shifts. My peers were still struggling to get their associates to engage, but my leadership began to stand out.

It's important to note that Jesus went through various stages and levels of suffering during His life on earth. Each trial proceeded the level of power and authority required for His next assignment. In this we can see that suffering is not a one-time experience. There is a price to pay for advancement and elevation in our lives. My situation unfolded with great suffering in my first marriage for which God provided a wonderfully blessed second marriage and family. I suffered in my career and God blessed and elevated my career to levels beyond my dreams. During these painful experiences, I chose to get closer to God. I ran to Him, not away from Him. It was my decision to fall into God's arms and rely on Him that caused my situations to turn. Sometimes people blame God for problems or pain that arises in their lives. This causes them to separate from the only way out of their situation.

The enemy wants us to crumble under the pressure of trials and tribulation. God's plan is for us to use these times to build our character and our trust in Him. When we are successful in enduring a trail or testing, we receive promotion. Just like students advance to the next grade level in school by taking and passing tests, God wants us to continue to pass the test and advance to the next level. The devil hopes that you will turn around, back up, cave in, or quit. He does not want God's people to continue to overcome and advance like Jesus did. God is committed to us, If we fail the test of suffering, He will allow us to retake the test so that we can put into practice the lessons we learned on how to overcome.

Jesus endured suffering with full knowledge of His Sonship. This was important because He never allowed the question of "is God with Me" to enter His mind. Other than the moment Jesus was separated from God by our sin, He never questioned if God was with Him. Suffering as a son is different than someone who is unsure of their standing or status with God. Suffering with the mentality of a servant or a slave creates different expectations than those of a son. The framework of our identity makes all of the difference in our ability to endure and suffer successfully. This framework forms the understanding of the Kingdom essentials that are necessary for co-laboring with God.

As my thirtieth anniversary with the Home Depot approached God began to tug at my heart about it being time to close this chapter of my life and move on. I immediately thought about how wonderful everything was going at work. This was my dream job. I remember thinking, "I can't leave now." But, God's tugging at my heart got stronger. This was God's way of letting me know that my assignment had been completed at The Home Depot. I began to understand that God had a new assignment for me and with the assignment I would need a new level of power (ability to get things done). To prepare for this transition, I would need to remember what I had learned about trials and suffering.

We'll never permanently escape trouble, trials, and suffering until we get to heaven. Jesus told us "In this world you will have tribulation, but be of good cheer, I have overcome the world." We must learn to endure hardship in life while maintaining our joy. In fact, joy is a secret weapon for suffering hardships successfully.

LEVEL 10

Joy and Praise

One day, while I was still very depressed over the turmoil of my broken marriage, a coworker approached me to talk. I was busy putting out various fires in the store but walking in love meant taking time to listen to others. He shared that he was going through some problems in his marriage, and he didn't know what to do. I had known this coworker for many years. We were good friends and even went to the same church for a while. I had not shared much of what I was going through in my marriage with him. He told me the issues they were facing as a couple and that it looked like they were heading towards divorce. I began to share my situation, as well. We were in the same boat, working at the same store and trusting God to help us with our problems.

As we shared stories, the conversation became heavier and heavier. The more we conversed about our situation, the more hopeless our cases sounded. I was beginning to feel even worse than I had before we started sharing. Then I stopped and said, "Wait, we're just rehearsing the problem." Sharing our sad stories didn't help either of us. We needed to do something to change what was going on. I told my friend to meet me behind the building during our next break. My plan was for us to meet behind the store and pray for our marriages. As I walked towards the back of the store, I heard the Lord speak to my heart, "You need to give praise for the answers to prayers that you have already prayed."

My friend arrived at the back of the building, and it was cold outside. There were no trucks waiting to be unloaded by the receiving team, so we were all alone. "Let's pray and give praise," I told my friend. Immediately, I started praying. He watched me for a moment, and then he joined in. As soon as he joined in, I began to praise God for hearing and helping us. I began to shout how thankful I was for God's promises and His faithfulness towards us. I began to act like my prayers had already been answered. I started jumping up and down and clapping my hands. My friend was still praying almost to himself, and I was acting like someone had set me on fire. It would have looked funny to someone if they had walked outside and saw us, but I didn't care. I remembered going to Super Bowl XXXIV in Atlanta. I had tickets and I was super excited. We had an ice storm in Atlanta but that did not quench my excitement. I had worked concessions at Superbowl XXVIII, but I had never been to a Super Bowl as a fan. If I needed any additional incentive to be hyped up, my favorite team; the St. Louis Rams was playing against the Tennessee Titans. The game had plenty of die-hard fans from both teams. I saw so many costumes and painted faces; it could have passed for Halloween night.

If you remember this game, it had one of the most exciting endings of all time. The game was full of ebbs and flows with several lead changes. We spent the fourth quarter standing on our feet. The crowd would roar for every score and third down conversion. Everyone in the stadium was standing to see what was going on. The game came down to the last play. The Tennessee Titans were driving for the game winning score, with the final seconds ticking off the clock. The Rams stopped the Titans wide receiver less than a yard away from the goal line. The game went down to the last tackle to preserve the victory for the Rams. The stadium erupted as the final seconds ran off the clock. Rams' fans were jumping around, dancing, and spinning around hugging one another. It was a great experience!

I will never forget the joy and exuberance that the fans expressed during the game. I yelled and screamed at the top of my lungs to support my team. That day I told myself that I would never give God less than I had given my favorite team. After all that He had done for me, I would never sit on my hands during praise service again.

I remembered cheering for the Rams, as I stood behind the store, praying for God's intervention. My friend must have thought I was going overboard but it didn't matter. After about 15 minutes, we were almost frozen, so we went back inside. As the warmth began to return to my fingers and toes, I noticed that I did not feel depressed like I had only minutes earlier. Nothing in my immediate situation had changed that I could tell, but I felt hopeful that it would. Instead of dwelling on the current mess of my life, I began thinking about what could be in my future.

This change of perspective was huge. Walking around all day, hopeful for good things to happen, was a lot easier and lighter than focusing on doom and gloom. Expressing joy was like taking a vitamin for my emotional state. Until now, I spent most of my prayer time petitioning God for help and in quiet reflection. After this, I began to spend time thanking and praising Him. I was jumping for joy, spinning around my house, like I had won the lottery every day. The more time that I spent focused on praise and thankfulness, the less worried, sad, and depressed I felt. It wasn't always easy to start praising God and thinking about the good things He had done. I made up my mind to do it whether I felt like it or not.

Capacity Expansion

I did not fully understand what was taking place at the time, but I had put a spiritual principle in place. Isaiah 61 records the mission of Jesus's ministry and the reason He was sent. Verse 3 states, "To appoint unto them that mourn in Zion, to give them beauty for ashes, the oil of joy for mourning, the garment of praise for the spirit of heaviness." The garment or mantle of praise was provided to get rid of a spirit of heaviness. This verse described what I was experiencing. The weight and sadness of my situation lifted when I spent time in praise. I would feel the pain of my broken heart throughout the day, but I began to feel joy after a time of praising God.

This scripture contains two powerful tools for believers—the oil of joy and the garment of praise. For me to remain consistent in my love walk at work, I needed help. I could maintain my focus on love for a while, but I would begin to feel depleted after several hours passed. You could say I was running out of fuel. I would go and recharge and refuel during my lunch break, but I needed more endurance. I needed my love tank to expand.

In the Gospels, Jesus talked about wine skins and new wine. You cannot pour new wine into old wine skins because the wine would expand, and the old wine skins, having lost their elasticity, would burst. It would ruin the wine skins and the wine would be lost as well. This parable of truth applies to us as vessels of God's love and power. Our spiritual capacity to receive and hold God's influence can diminish if we remain in sorrow and grief for extended periods. While grief and loss are a part of life, we are not supposed to camp out there. People who stay in a downcast mindset invite the enemy to layer on oppression and a host of other unfavorable conditions.

One way to protect the elasticity of the wine skin was by applying oil. The oil would condition the leather skins and allow them to remain expandable. A second step that would extend the life of the wine skin was to cover it or protect it from being dried out by the sun. The oil of joy is the perfect solution for feelings of sadness, despair, grief, and loss. Sorrow and suffering cannot exist in the presence of joy; they have to leave. Joy is different from happiness. Happiness is based on conditions being pleasant or enjoyable. Joy is anchored in the promises of God's word.

I shifted my focus to what God had promised me as His child. I rejoiced that: He promised never to leave me or forsake me (Deuteronomy 31:8), He came to heal the broken hearted (Isaiah 61:1), and He is able to do exceedingly, abundantly above all that I could ask or imagine (Ephesians 3:20). I decided to make my response based on His promises and not my feelings or condition. In my mind, I saw my finances changed, my relationship restored, and my career thriving. I based my response on the evidence of His word. This is the essence of faith.

Have you ever watched ducks on a lake during a storm? They do not seem bothered by the rain at all. God has given them a protective covering on their feathers to keep them dry and warm. They can remain comfortable in downpours that send other animals running for cover. This is where the saying, "Like water off of a duck's back," comes from. A garment of praise represents a mantle or covering over us. God's presence covers the life of those who remain in a position of praise. It's a supernatural representation of the natural protection that God has given ducks. When we make praise a consistent focus and our usual response to challenges, we remain steady during the storms of life.

Mourning and heaviness from pain and loss were drying up and shrinking my capacity to operate in love and kindness. God had provided the oil of joy to condition my heart and the garment of praise to cover and protect it from exposure. This combination increased the capacity of my love tank. I began to make joy and praise a consistent part of my time with God daily. This change of focus caused things to shift into high gear.

Tapping into joy and praise gave me the strength to walk in love continuously. Performing the royal walk was never too taxing when my joy level was full. Associate concerns didn't wear on my patience, and I addressed customer complaints almost effortlessly. Performing at this level of giving to others was impossible on my own. Joy had become strength that allowed me to endure. We can access the joy that comes from the Lord. We do this when we create a continuous or consistent environment of praise and thanksgiving.

"Do not be dejected and sad, for the joy of the Lord is your strength." — Nehemiah 8:10 NLT

The Bible is full of instruction on joy. James 1:2 tells us to consider it pure joy when we face trials of many kinds. Jesus said, "In this world, you will have tribulation, but be of good cheer, I have overcome the world."

One of my favorite examples of the power of praise during difficult times is the account of Paul and Silas in Acts 16:20-27. Paul and Silas were whipped and put into the inner prison for preaching the Gospel. Stocks were locked onto their feet. At midnight Paul and Silas prayed and sang praises to God, and the other prisoners heard them. Suddenly an earthquake shook the foundations of the prison, causing all the cell doors to open. These men were set free from physical chains and shackles by praising God.

After being whipped and put into prison, Paul and Silas could have complained about it. But they chose to praise God instead of feeling sorry for themselves or being angry at the authorities. They didn't wait until they felt good or something good happened. These men used their praise to produce the joy of the Lord. The joy of the Lord changed their situation and made them glad. We can learn from their example to not allow our emotional state to dictate our response.

As I shared in the previous chapter, Jesus knew firsthand about suffering and tribulations. Yet, Jesus instructs His followers to focus on the peace found in Him and be of good cheer during troubled times. It is the force of joy in our lives that will allow us to endure suffering successfully and overcome. Jesus endured death on a cross because of the joy set before Him (Hebrews 12:2).

Jesus focused on His mission, the billions of souls that would be saved from destruction. He focused on our deliverance as His life drained down the cross onto the hill of Calvary. Securing our Salvation meant enough for Jesus to endure separation from His Father. During His previous trials, Jesus remained in connection and fellowship with God. The act of Jesus taking on the sin of the whole world dictated that God turn His back on Jesus. For the first time in eternity Jesus was isolated, cut off from God. He was made a curse in exchange for us receiving the blessing. You and I walking in the blessing of fellowship with God was Jesus' goal. This blessing was made possible by the joy that allowed Jesus to complete the mission.

Jesus knew what was at stake and what was to be gained by His obedience to death. Jesus' joy came from knowing what was being made available, not His circumstances. Likewise, we must tap into the truth of our situation, not our circumstances. When we face trials, the truth is that we are not alone. The truth is that God has the final say, and He has already spoken good concerning every area of our lives. It is our responsibility to understand these promises and respond in joy to what we know.

Joy and praise provide a habitation for God's presence. Abiding in His presence provides us with endless advantages. These advantages are not limited to religious or spiritual applications; they include our lives in the marketplace as well. The level of wisdom operating in my life increased once praise became a way of life. The understanding that I am referring to has nothing to do with my knowledge, experience, or IQ. Things that I did not know or understand, answers that I did not have, would come into my thoughts. I could not take credit for it. I would praise God for the answer or solution and put it into action.

Use the Proper Tools

Joy and praise are keys to suffering successfully. Remember that God has not forgotten about you or your situation. The worst thing we can do during tough times is to complain. Complaining is a way of using the power of your words, negatively. When you repeat the bad things that happen in your life, you are reinforcing them. When God delivered the children of Israel from Egypt, there were a series of remarkable miracles involved. Yet, negative attitudes and complaining caused them to wander in the wilderness rather than enter the promised land.

God gave the children of Israel manna from heaven when they needed food. Yet, they complained that they didn't have meat. God sent them quail for meat (Exodus 16:1-12) but that wasn't enough. They complained and accused God of taking them into the desert to kill them. The Israelites murmured and complained every step of the way. Their refusal to put complaining and murmuring behind them forfeited their access into the promised land. If you know the story, God waited until that generation died in the wilderness, then He took their children into the promised land.

It's normal to want to express ourselves when we are hurting. We are better off sharing our feelings with God and asking for His help. I am not saying that other people cannot assist us during trials. Perry Smith was a Godsend for me. He understood my situation and did not gossip about it. Perry gave me Godly counsel. He refused to allow me to feel sorry for myself and would not reinforce my negative feelings. Sometimes sharing with the wrong people will make a bad situation worse.

Choose joy and praise. You do not need anything or anyone that does not align with these. As we co-labor with God we are sure to face trials and uncomfortable situations. We must remember to count it all joy and offer a sacrifice of praise to access God's provision for these situations.

LEVEL 11

Kingdom Essentials

"Being essential" means that someone or something is absolutely necessary and extremely important. What I am sharing with you qualifies as essential information. God has made Kingdom principles available to anyone desiring to achieve their best life. We cannot expect to reach the full potential of our lives without the author of life. To operate in Kingdom principles requires that we adopt a Kingdom mindset. Being essential in our sphere of influence is a result of possessing God's mindset and using His principals to advance His agenda in the area He has assigned.

Kingdom principles work in any field, industry, or geographic area, regardless of the economic or political environment. The world is facing problems and needs solutions that require Kingdom Essential People to step forward. Developing the right mindset is priority.

While there are practical steps to take, I think it brings better clarity to look at it as stages of development. Becoming the essential leaders that God desires in the marketplace requires that we have the proper identity, develop His divine nature, and understand the importance of process. We must know who we are in Christ. As we develop in the nature of our Father, we can co-labor with Him. While salvation happens instantaneously, there is a process of development into Sonship. As we mature in our walk, we receive assignments that require us to operate in Sonship. Armed with this internal blueprint, we have the foundation for exploits in every area of society.

Identity

The moment we accept Christ into our lives, a transformation happens. It is the greatest miracle that can ever be performed. We are transitioned from spiritual death to eternal life and delivered from the curse of the law into the blessing of Abraham.

> *"If any man is in Christ, he is a new creation, old things*
> *have passed away; behold all things have become new."*
> 2 Corinthians 5:17

All our past present and future mistakes or sins are separated from us, and we stand before God as if we never sinned. Our spotless standing before God is based on Jesus, not our merit. The perfect walk has been completed by the perfect life that Jesus lived as our sacrifice. The work of accepting by faith Jesus' accomplishments is our responsibility.

The most essential step is to transition from a "doing" mentality to a heart motivation of "being." Our identity or knowing who we are is the basis for this change. The proper identity must be firmly established to develop in God's nature and collaborate or co-labor with Him. God does not want servants. He desires sons/daughters who follow His lead.

Identity begins with our self-perception. How we see ourselves, what we believe, expect, speak, and say about ourselves is vital. An example of how poor self-perception can disqualify people of God occurred, when God sent Joshua, Caleb, and the ten spies to survey the promised land (Numbers 13:30-32). Twelve people were selected for the assignment, one to represent each tribe of Israel.

Ten of the representatives came back with what God called an evil report. This poor self-perception led to a chain of events that resulted in that generation of people forfeiting their right to enter the promised land. They died in the wilderness. Forty years later, Joshua and Caleb led their children into the promised land.

We gain our Kingdom Identity through Christ, not our own performance, abilities, economic, or social status. It is just as detrimental to think beneath our Kingdom status as it is to ascribe our status based on our merit. When we realize who we are in Christ it paves the foundation for our lives. As a child, Jesus studied the Scriptures to find out who He was. At the age of twelve, Jesus discussed the Law with the Scribes and Priests. Jesus was paving the foundation for the life that He was called to live after years of studying the Scriptures. His understanding of His identity was critical to the Father activating Him into ministry.

We cannot skip the step of learning who we are from the Word of God. Without allowing the Word to establish a new blueprint for us, we will get caught up in who we used to be. Our old habits, memories, and past mistakes will try to convince us that we are undeserving of God's blessing. The devil will try to remind us of our past lives to keep us confined in our mindsets. He does not want us walking in righteousness and authority. One of the enemy's oldest tricks is to try to convince us that God's promises will not work or do not apply to us. Even when we see the evidence in the lives of others, the devil wants you to think that it will not happen for you.

I remember being covered up with financial debt and hearing people share how God stepped in and delivered them. The devil quickly began to whisper, "It happened for them, but it won't happen for you." Because I had made financial mistakes and some bad decisions, the devil tried to convince me that God would not deliver me from my self-inflicted wounds.

There was a time that I had over $30,000 in credit card debt. At the time, this debt represented well over half of my annual salary. I was also facing Federal Tax Penalties that if fully levied would be an additional $30,000. Until I realized who I was to God, I was in doubt that He would intervene on my behalf. I listened to the enemy and felt shame for the mistakes that I had made. For a while, I was afraid that the IRS would press charges and that I would be sent to jail. This began to torment me. I actually had dreams of being sent to jail for tax penalties.

I thank God for His timely mercy and grace that I came to experience through listening to my pastor's teaching on being justified and declared the righteousness of God. The following two scriptures became important to my identity formation as I mediated on their truth of who God's Word says that I am:

> *"God made him who had no sin to be sin for us, so that in him we might be made the righteousness of God, — 2 Corinthians 5:21*

> *"Since we have been justified through faith, we have peace with God through our Lord Jesus Christ." — Romans 5:1*

Being made righteous in His sight means we are in right standing with Him, without guilt or condemnation. Because of my faith in Jesus, God sees me "Just as if I had never committed sin."

Armed with this truth, I began to release my faith for God to heal and restore my finances. I reminded God of His promise to supply all my needs. I confessed what the Word promised about His provision for my life. I had to use the promises from the Word to dominate the negative thoughts from the enemy. Speaking the truth of the Word eliminates the worry and dread that the enemy uses to attack us. Gaining understanding that God was not holding my faults against me was huge. The revelation that I was faultless in His sight because of Jesus gave me the courage to ask and expect Him to intervene on my behalf.

In time, I was able to pay off all my debts and I have remained debt free. Through God's wisdom and favor, the IRS bill was reduced to $3,000! I remember the day that I paid it off. I laughed at the devil who had tormented me with dreams of going to jail and I praised God for His faithfulness. I later found out that criminal charges were not applicable in my situation. This was a lie from the devil that I entertained and allowed him to use against me.

Just as Jesus studied the Word to discover His identity, I had to make the Word my priority to renew my mind. As I began to understand the truth about who I was, I began to see myself the way God sees me. This is our proper identity. It is important to remember that to overestimate ourselves or underestimate ourselves is a dangerous place to be. This posture allows the enemy ground to make his attacks upon our identity.

I initially attempted to achieve success on my own. My focus was on my performance. Relying on hard work, education, and my ability to get results failed. After years of toiling under the burden of performance, I tried thinking my way to success. Networking, building a professional image, identifying people by their personality traits were all good things to know but they did not deliver what I was after. Even after I rededicated my life to Christ, I seemed to be spinning my wheels where my career and finances were concerned.

All of this was puzzling to me. When I was ignoring God and doing my own thing, I knew that I was out of bounds and out of His will. When I came to myself and recommitted my life to Him, I expected to see an external change accompany the internal transformation. "Where was the blessing that covered the life of a believer?" I thought. I initially placed confidence in my hands to perform or "do" what it took to get ahead. After that, my confidence was in my head to know the ways to success. I spent years focused on my hands and my head without engaging my heart. My heart was preoccupied by selfish motives.

The doing of our hands (performance) and the knowing in our minds (knowledge) are not our source. They are however, meant to be used as evidence of God living in and working through us. Only as we abide in Christ is our identity as His beloved sons/daughters nurtured and strengthened. This is our true identity.

"It is in Him that we live and move and have our being."
— *Acts 17:28*

In the wilderness, Jesus was tempted by the devil in two areas. First, the devil tried to question Jesus' understanding of His identity ... "If thou be the Son of God ..." Next, the devil tempted Jesus with a shortcut to the process of the glory promised. The devil told Jesus that all the kingdoms of the world would be given to Jesus if He chose to bow down to the devil and worshipped him instead of suffering on the Cross as our atonement.

After all these years, the enemy is still using the same tricks and ploys. Unfortunately, in many cases, these tricks are still being effective in causing believers to stumble. If you have not already been tested in these areas of identity and process, it is highly likely that you will be.

Proper identity is essential to being who God has called you to be. You cannot be essential to God's Kingdom without knowing who you are. So often people pursue the will of God for their lives with their hands and head without first settling the heart issue. We must step into being the beloved sons and daughters of God before we run off to tackle an assignment.

Slave, Servant, and Son

Identity transformation consists of three stages: from a slave to a servant, then a son. Before I rededicated my life to Christ, I was a slave to my impulses and fears. The pride of life and lust for things dictated my focus. I placed the highest value on my reputation, status, and money. I had knowledge of God and His Word, but I did not expect any help from Him. God honors our insistence to go our own way. He does not force Himself upon us. How prideful I was to think that I could accomplish anything of substance, without God. There I was, thinking that my education, connections, and hard work were all that I needed.

I entered into toil, strenuous, fatiguing labor for extended lengths of time. This mindset was due to my estranged relationship with God.

> *"... remember that at that time you were separate from Christ, excluded from citizenship in Israel and foreigners to the covenants of promise, without hope and without God in the world. ... You live in this world without God and without hope." — Ephesians 2:12*

After years of beating my head against a proverbial brick wall, I came to my senses. I had drifted so far from who I knew I was supposed be, that I did not recognize myself. I had become self-absorbed, deceptive, and manipulating. I was trying so hard to advance myself that I was rarely concerned with anyone else. I was empty inside. I felt alone regardless of who was around. I had set out to prove that I could make it on my own and that I did not need God. This experiment failed. One day I looked at my reflection in my bathroom mirror and said, "That's enough!" I recommitted my heart to Christ that day.

The emptiness that I had tried unsuccessfully to fill with the pursuit of money and status, was now being filled. At this point I realized that my life was tied to Christ forever. He was the only thing that filled the hole left in my heart from being rejected by my earthly father. His love was healing the hurt from my broken past. All the effort and money that I spent trying to achieve peace left me with frustration. There was no substitute for His peace, and it came free of charge.

I began to read my bible and pray. I started going to church and heard people from various departments asking for volunteers to serve. Wanting to show God that I was sincere about my commitment to Him, I signed up for as many things as I could. It made sense to me that if I was faithful concerning things important to God, then He would be faithful towards me. Eventually, I settled on serving in children's ministry. I enjoyed it so much that I began taking classes to become a minister. These decisions resulted in my relationship with God becoming priority. I determined that I would faithfully serve God and earn the blessings that He promised.

My career showed modest improvement, I was finally promoted to the role of Assistant Manager. Adopting the identity as a servant of God directed me towards some of the same behaviors I previously upheld. I passionately believed, that if I was faithful, then I would reap a harvest. If I prayed and read my Bible, then God would be pleased, and His favor would show up for me. I worked just as hard as I had under the slave mentality. Only now, I was working as unto God and not man. It was during this phase of my walk that I received the instructions to walk in love as a lifestyle. I embraced these instructions as love and kindness revolutionized my life. With my focus on earning Gods favor with my love walk, I was still on a roller coaster of good weeks and not so good weeks.

The challenge with living with the servant's identity was that it still had the attachment to performance. I had to do the right things at work and finish each task with excellence. Anything less would cause me to feel like I had failed to keep my end of the deal. This meant, I was diminishing my blessings from God. If I did not wake up early enough to pray and spend time with God before work, I was unsure how the day would transpire. I was responsible for multiple departments within the store. I tried to do everything right. Yet, I was still worrying how the Associate's performance might impact my standing with the company and even with God. I was confident that my salvation was secure but the blessing on my life seemed yet to be determined. Living with a servant's mentality was better than being a slave to fear, with days full of toil. But I wondered how long before I would earn a real breakthrough. I often worried about how many times would I build up favor then make a mistake and have to start over.

The servant mentality appears to be supported by scripture. One of my favorite passages in the bible is found in the Book of Deuteronomy 28.

"Now if you faithfully obey the voice of the Lord your God and are careful to follow all His commandments, I am

giving you today, the Lord your God will set you high above the nations of the earth. And all these blessings will come upon you and overtake you if you will obey the voice of the Lord your God. — *Deuteronomy 28:1-2*

These verses are followed by an extensive list of blessings that cover every area of life. This listing of blessings continues until verse 15 which states "If however, you do not obey the Lord your God by carefully following all His commandments and statues I am giving you today, all these curses will come upon you and overtake you." This verse is followed by a list of curses that cover every area of life.

This Old Testament scripture and several others gives the basis for the servant identity. Here the relationship with God is presented as a conditional agreement. If we do certain things, then He will do certain things. For decades, Christians have believed and lived their lives under this performance-based mindset. I was taught and believed it as well.

The problem with applying this and other Old Testament scriptures to our lives today is proper context. This was written for people who did not have relationship with God through Jesus and His sacrifice. Before Jesus, people were expected to serve God and follow the commandments to receive His blessings. These commands included the Ten Commandments as well as hundreds of additional ceremonial laws.

Under this Old Covenant, no one was able to successfully keep all the laws and commandments. Every year the high priest had to make animal sacrifices for himself and the people. Jesus came and lived the perfect life and fulfilled every detail of the Law. He then offered His spotless life as a sacrifice for all sin. His death took care of sin in our past, present and future. Through faith in Jesus, we are invited to become sons and daughters of God.

"Behold the Lamb of God who takes away the sin of the whole world." — *John 1:29*

God's new design for our relationship with Him is Sonship not servanthood. This is the New Covenant. It's clearly presented in scripture.

> *"The Spirit you have received does not make you slaves so that you live in fear again; but rather the Spirit you received brought about your adoption to sonship. And by Him we cry Abba, Father." — Romans 8:15*

Romans 8:15 does not mention anything about servanthood or transitioning from slavery into anything but Sonship. God's plan was for Jesus's sacrifice to bring us into His family as adopted sons and daughter as we are led by the Spirit.

> *"For as many as are led by the spirit of God, these are the sons of God." — Romans 8:14*

The Word of God contrasts our condition before salvation. Before salvation, we are chained to slave status and fear, with adoption and Sonship becoming our new status once we receive Christ.

> *"We are brought out of darkness into His wonderful light." — 1 Peter 2:9*

Being adopted and made heirs, confers permanent legal status as a member of the family. We are not expected to work to earn God's love, favor, or blessings. When I think of my own children, they do not question or try to earn their status as my offspring. They don't perform to maintain their status. When it's time to eat, they do not consider how they have performed or behaved, they take their seat at the table fully expecting to receive. Despite my human failings, I receive my children without performance or qualifiers. How much more does our Heavenly Father accept us, and remain in love with us? He is the perfect Father.

Now if we are children, then we are heirs of God and co-heirs with Christ, if indeed we share in His sufferings that we may also share in His glory. — Romans 8:17

When we accept Christ by faith, we can receive His peace regarding our position in the family of God. We receive our adoption as sons/daughters of God by faith. Faith is simply expressing confidence in God and His word. This is our identity, and we must accept who we are to God and have it settled in our hearts. Another way to describe this confidence is to rest in our identity. As I mentioned before, a slave's mindset leads to toil and a servant's mindset leads to labor. As God's son, we must learn to rest in our identity. We must stop trying to earn God's favor and accumulate points to cash in for a blessing. Rather, we are to take God at His word and by faith believe that we are His beloved children adopted through the blood of Christ. This position of resting in confidence of our Sonship is the first phase of the kingdom essential mindset.

A son will rest from the striving to make something happen through performance and striving for approval, acceptance, and access to the blessings of God. Rest is not becoming lazy or a lack of productivity, but rather a lifestyle of co-laboring with God. The focus is on being developed in His nature and aligned with His assignment for our lives through abiding daily in Him as our source. Our goal should be to take our position as an heir fully developed in love (the Divine Nature), accepting the role of serving others, in order that a reproduction of God's nature would occur in our assigned area of influence.

The Divine Nature

God's desire for us is to take on His nature and represent Him in our spheres of influence. God wants us to co-labor with Him as Jesus did. This is the highest result of our relationship with Him. Jesus told His disciples that He is dependent on God and the Father living in Him is responsible for the "works" or miracles being performed.

> *"The son can do nothing by Himself, he can only do what he sees the Father doing." — John 5:19*

> *"Don't you believe that I am in the Father, and the Father is in me? The words I say to you I do not speak of my own authority. Rather, it is the Father, living in me, who is doing His work." — John 14:10*

Having unhealthy desires for anything constitutes lust. It may take the form of power, money, fame, houses, cars, or a person. When that desire occupies your heart, your heart becomes corrupted. My pursuit of promotion, money and recognition corrupted my heart at the beginning of my career. The lust for success was the basis for my performance driven life. Lust is not only associated with sex. Lust is a strong desire for anything opposed to God's nature. It can be anything that takes up residence in our heart and draws our affection and attention away from God.

When I finally exhausted myself trying to achieve fulfillment and success by my own methods, I became convinced of my need for Christ. Every form of self-indulgence that I tried failed to deliver. I thank God that I finally realized that going harder and faster after those things would not change the result. I would still be left empty and alone. Lust instills a hunger that cannot be satisfied by pursuing or obtaining the things you lust for. Our hearts can only be truly satisfied with the peace that Christ gives.

> *"I am leaving you with a gift-peace of mind and heart. And the peace I give is a gift the world cannot give. So, do not be troubled or afraid." — John 14:27*

What God did in my life and career was nothing short of a miracle. Everything that I was chasing after but never grasping, started to flow into my life. God gave me better desires and then exceeded my expectations within those areas when my desire changed from acquiring things for myself, to loving and giving.

The key is allowing the blueprint of the new nature to be imprinted on our hearts. This causes us to receive the mind of Christ. Our ways become submitted to His ways. His thoughts become our thoughts. His desire for our lives becomes our passion and burden. This is a departure from the Old Testament, made possible through Jesus. In the Old Testament we find the understanding that God's thoughts are not our thoughts, and His ways are much higher than our ways (see Isaiah 55: 8-9).

In the New Covenant we are invited to receive the nature, thoughts, and ways of God through Jesus. God has a plan for us to participate or collaborate in the divine nature.

"For who can know the Lord's thoughts? Who knows enough to teach him? But we understand these things, for we have the mind of Christ." — *1 Corinthians 2:16*

"But you have an anointing from the Holy One and you know all things." — *1 John 2:20*

"Through these he has given us His very great and precious promises so that through them you might participate in the divine nature, having escaped the corruption in the world caused by lust." — *2 Peter 1:4*

"Let this mind be in you which was also in Christ Jesus. Who being in the form of God thought it not robbery to be equal with God." — *Philippians 2:5-6*

As we partake of the Divine Nature, we are no longer separated from His wisdom. This new level of access to God and His wisdom is made available through Jesus so that we can co-labor with God as Jesus did. Tapping into God's wisdom leads us into God-sized results and helps us navigate through the required processes.

Engaging the Process

When I rededicated my life to Christ, I was made aware of how spiritually bankrupt I had become. In addition to being selfish and prideful, I had become deceitful and callous. I begin to lie and curse with every breath. It began while I was trying to boost my image by adding small lies. Before long I would lie for no reason at all. I told so many lies that I would forget which lies I told people. When God showed me who I had become, it broke me.

Walking in my new life with Christ meant putting away those things that were not like Him. I had no idea how I was going to stop lying and cursing. They had become automatic for me. I did not want to go through the process of feeling guilty every time I told a lie or cursed. My behavior was not in line with the character God was requiring. I wanted to please God, but I knew that change would not happen on my own.

I prayed and told God that I was through with that life, and I wanted to please Him. I asked Him to take away from me all the things that were not pleasing to Him. He placed a desire in me to read the Bible and to pray. Every day, before I did anything else, I was dedicated to praying and reading. It was a hunger or desire just like wanting to eat breakfast every day. In fact, I would not eat breakfast until I had prayed and read my Bible. On my days off of work, I would spend hours sitting on the floor reading and meditating on the scriptures. I was not sure what was happening but as I immersed myself in prayer and the Word, the lying and cursing stopped. It was not a result of my focus on telling the truth or speaking differently. By embracing Him, my behavior changed. It was God working in me causing me to do what pleased Him (see Philippians 2:13).

His internal desires will cause a change in our behavior and old things will pass away because the new life has come. We can get caught up on trying to produce behavior modification without the internal process. Behavioral modification is a work of the mind or body that leads to frustration and defeat. When we come to God and spend time in His Word and in His presence, He begins to cause us to will and do that which is His pleasure.

There are internal and external processes that take place during our development. While we are being developed in the nature of God our spirit man must grow and develop. The internal process is the development and growth of our spirit. Spiritual growth is not always tied to the amount of time that someone has been a believer or a Christian. Growth in any type of life form requires nourishment. Plants, animals, people, anything that is alive must be fed to continue to live and to thrive. The spirit inside of us is no different. Our spirit represents who we really are, it's the part of us that is eternal. We are spirits who have a mind/soul and live in a physical body. Just as we feed our body with food and our minds with information, we must feed our spirit.

As new believers we are told to desire the milk of the Word to help us grow (see 1Peter 2:2). The Bible is the milk that provides nourishment for our spirit. Reading and meditating on the truth of God's word strengthens our inner man. Internalizing the Word will cause our spirit man to grow. If you haven't already begun, find a version of the Bible that you can understand and begin reading it daily. It does not matter how small the amount of time you begin with, focus on being consistent. Under normal conditions, not one of us would go a full day without eating natural food. The same concept applies for our spirit. We need to be fed daily.

There is also a need to be taught the Word of God. Paul tells one of the early churches that they were behind in their development and ability to digest solid spiritual food (see 1Corinthians 3:2). Just as an infant begins with milk but progresses to solid foods, we are expected to develop. If a human being were fed a milk only diet for years, they would start to have some developmental problems. Failure to nurture our spirit leads to our lives being directed by our unrenewed minds. Putting the Word in action in our everyday lives causes maturity in the divine nature.

Galatians 5:22 gives us a blueprint of the areas that we should be developed in. It begins with love. Love is the essence of the divine nature. God is love. When we are born again, God places His spirit on the inside of us. The spirit of love on the inside of us produces joy, peace, patience, goodness, kindness, faithfulness, gentleness, and self-control.

When we engage in the process of growth and developing the divine nature, old behaviors and habits do not fit us anymore. Our spirits become stronger than the desires of our minds and bodies. We begin to escape the lust of the world and give Christ preeminence in our hearts.

As we endure the process of growing in God's nature our lives reflect His love. This does not mean as soon as we receive salvation, we can ask for the CEO position in our companies and get it the next month. There is a love-based process that we go through to prepare for each level of elevation and increase in our lives. What kind of Father would I be if I handed my 11-year-old child the keys to my car because they said they want to drive? I would be placing them and others in danger. My love for my child requires that I allow the process of growth and development to occur before I grant that request.

> "Now I say, the heir, as long as he is a child, does not differ
> at all from a servant, though he is lord of the entire estate."
> — Galatians 4:1.

Delayed growth or development will cause us to experience delays in our elevation. This is not a punishment but rather a loving decision for our own good. Elevation reveals the heart of a person. Money is an amplifier. Money causes whatever is in our heart to increase. When I began my lifestyle of love and kindness, I did not have the ability to give anything financially. That's why God reminded me that kindness was free. After developing a heart for others, my financial resources began to increase. I began showing kindness by paying for the order of the people in the car behind me in Starbucks' drive thru. As I continued to focus on others my finances and career continued to improve. I went from showing kindness through words and deeds to generously giving people things like cars and houses. The increase in my finances amplified what was in my heart.

Imagine what would have happened if I received the same levels of promotion while my heart was full of selfishness and pride? I would have destroyed my career and possibly my life. God was working on me while He was working for me. The external process is just as important as the internal. While I was growing and developing in the Divine Nature, God was orchestrating the leadership structure around me. He provided mentors for me to learn from and pattern myself after. The leadership of the company went through several changes from the CEO position down. Leaders who valued integrity and servant leadership were placed in key positions.

God exposed me to several different store environments before placing me at the Cascade store. This gave me a vision for what a store could achieve for its associates and community. While all of this was going on, I had to trust that He was taking care of everything. At the time, I could not see all of the connections and adjustments that He was doing on my behalf. Developing trust in His process was just as important as developing His nature. At the perfect time, my nature aligned with the assignment He had for me and promotion came. Because I endured the process, I experienced several levels of promotion. It never changed my heart for people but rather allowed me to grow in my ability to impact others.

Understanding this essential mindset will help you prepare for and optimize the assignments for your future. Focusing on the right identity, developing in God's nature, and having patience through the process will make you essential to His Kingdom.

The Call to Sonship

Since Jesus' resurrection from the dead, the invitation to join the family of God has been available. Throughout the age of the church, the picture of our place in God's family has become clearer and clearer. Now more than ever, there is a need to understand that believers are being called, beckoned, even commanded to take our place as sons and daughters. God is waiting for us as His sons and daughters to awaken to our identity and take our proper places. The Father's call is for us to be matured in His nature and aligned with His assignment for our lives. These assignments cover every sector of society. The whole creation echoes the Father's call as a cry for the revealing of the sons of God.

"For the eagerly awaiting creation waits for the revealing of the sons of God." — Romans 8:19

All of creation cries out for the revealing of those who have been transformed by love, who co-labor with the Father to bring solutions, elevation, cures, inventions, and rest. The call goes out from the fields of education, business, government, family, arts and entertainment, media, and the church.

The need for Sonship has been established and God has provided access to our change of status.

"And because you are sons, God sent the spirit of His son into our hearts crying Abba Father." — Galatians 4:6

It is up to us to embrace the status that has been made available. The revealing or unveiling of Sonship happens within us. We must believe that we are called into Sonship. In Luke 15, Jesus told the story of the

Prodigal Son. The younger of two sons asked his father for his part of the inheritance in advance. After receiving his inheritance, the younger son went away and foolishly squandered it all away. Being destitute, he accepted a job feeding pigs. His situation was so dire that he wanted the pig's food for himself. The Bible says that he then *"came to himself."* He remembered that he was a son and that his father had servants who always had food to spare. His situation caused him to forget who he was because of his behavior and predicament. Selfish ambition and pride consumed him and led him to demand his inheritance. Shame and regret for his actions covered his mind after he lost everything he had. But one day he came to himself and remembered that he was a son. He returned to his father hoping to become a servant but was received with open arms as a son.

Past mistakes and failures do not nullify Sonship. When I wasted my stock portfolio and had nothing to show for it, the guilt and shame was heavy. God did not judge me by my mistakes, He only considered that Jesus had paid a dear price to bring me back to Him. Once I came to myself and reached out to Him, He accepted me. He did not designate me to second class status, but as a fully vested son. I had to work through my bad beliefs that tied me to servant status, but God accepted me as a son. When I realized that God did not want me as His servant, I had to renew my mind to all that Sonship status changed (see Romans 12:1-2).

We cannot co-labor with God if we hold on to a servant's mindset. We must become sons who wholeheartedly serve in love. The servant mindset will keep us confined to the extent of our performance and failures. This containment of our focus reduces the area of our impact to inside the four walls of the church and a few select areas beyond them. This is largely due to fear as we seek to operate in the marketplace. Relying on our own abilities and performance opens us to this fear. We have been delivered from fear.

"There is no fear in love, but perfect love casts out fear: because fear has to do with punishment. The one who fears is not made perfect in love." — 1 John 4:18-19

Embracing love delivers us from fear. Every time fear shows up it should be a reminder that we have been delivered from it. We must refuse to fear and remain focused on God's love for us. Fear comes to make us focus on ourselves. When we place our focus on our own promotion, safety, or wellbeing, we are taking our eyes off God's love for us. Placing ourselves in the center of attention gives fear access into our lives. It serves us well to keep Romans 8:15 in our hearts.

For you have not received a spirit of slavery that returns you to fear, but you received the Spirit of Sonship by whom we cry Abba! Father. — Romans 8:15

The word Abba translated means "Daddy." When one of my children needs me, they call me Daddy not Father. While I am their father, the title sounds formal and distant compared to Daddy. God wants us in intimate relationship with Him to the extent that we call Him "Daddy" when we need Him.

Jesus only did what he saw His father doing. This shows the level of relationship they shared. We must become dependent on Him for our directions, strategy, and responses. The validation of Sonship is not in exploits, but rather in being led by God. As we are led by His Spirit, He provides the transformation, exploits, and miracles.

"For as many as are led by the spirit of God, these are the sons of God." — Romans 8:14

Co-laboring with God will produce transformation in your business, marriage, ministry, and career. Entire sectors of society will be impacted as sons and daughters respond to the call and show up.

All of creation is crying out for the revealing of those who have been transformed by love, who co-labor with the Father to bring solutions, elevation, cures, inventions, and rest. The call goes out from the fields of education, business, government, family, arts and entertainment, media, and the church. Have you come to yourself? Will you answer the call to Sonship?

LEVEL 12

KINDNESS, GENEROSITY, AND PHILANTHROPY

D eveloping our relationship with God and receiving His nature causes His attributes to show up in our lives. Having the communication level that allows us to receive specific instructions for our lives separates relationship from mere religion. My trials took me to the point where religious activity was of little value. I needed answers and understanding. My condition required strength that was not my own. While walking in this relationship, I received clear instructions that changed me at the core. My circumstances soon changed dramatically. I am forever grateful for the opportunity to develop a relationship with the Creator of the universe.

The most powerful thing in the universe is the Word of God. What He speaks and has spoken, His word ranks even higher than His name (Psalm 138:2). When acted upon, His Word establishes a foundation for success. When we respond to specific instructions that He shares with us, that foundation will support exponential growth or manifestation in our lives. The first miracle Jesus performed was turning water into wine. Preceding this miracle, His mother, Mary, told the servants, "Whatever he says to you, do it." Obeying the instructions of Christ was the recipe for the miracle. They could have ignored Him or failed to comply and missed out on the blessing. I am thankful that when

God told me to focus on love and kindness that I followed through. I experienced a miraculous transformation in my life as a result.

When God told me that "love gives" and that "kindness was free," it took all my excuses off the table. Following through had nothing to do with my lack of finances. Kindness is the currency of love, and I started sharing it with others. While it began with me sharing my heart with my associates and customers, it became contagious. Kindness infected every area of my life. When I went to the grocery store, I offered to take shopping carts back to the front of the store after people loaded their groceries. I spoke kind words to cashiers and complimented people on their appearance. The impact that these simple actions had on people was incredible. I was empowered to brighten people's day by simply showing kindness.

Going out of my way on behalf of others became my personal goal. I saw this example in the story of the Good Samaritan (see Luke 10:25-37). Jesus shares this parable in response to a lawyer asking what qualifies a person to be my neighbor. Jesus shares the story of a man being robbed and beaten and left for dead. Religious people from this man's community passed by and saw him lying there. Instead of stopping to help him, they crossed to the other side of the road to avoid him. They went out of their way to avoid the poor man. Finally, a Samaritan who was a foreigner to the injured man stopped to help him. Verse 33 says that "He had compassion on him." Compassion means to have an awareness of the distress of others and to assist them. He did not just pity him; he went out of his way, spending time and money to help the stranger recover. Going out of my way to help others reminded me that people had done the same for me. Remembering the kindness shown to me makes me thankful for the opportunities to show kindness to others.

One of my earliest memories of someone going out of their way to help me was when I was ten years old. I was visiting my cousin for the Summer. We played on the playground at his school while his mother registered him for the upcoming school year. I smelled food and followed the scent to the cafeteria area. The school PTA was hosting a potluck to raise money for the upcoming school year. They were grilling all types of meat on a huge barrel grill outside the cafeteria. I went to the door of the school cafeteria and looked through the glass insert. There were rows of tables filled with all types of food and desserts. There was a table at the door where the people were purchasing tickets to enter. I did not have any money, so I went back to watch the man cook on the big grill. I had never seen a grill that size or so much meat on a grill at once. The man cooking the meat was trimming the fat off the end of a massive slab of meat. I thought to myself, what if I asked him to let me have the piece that he cut off? I was afraid to ask a stranger such a request, but I was hungry. As I was summoning my courage to ask, another gentleman standing nearby turned to me and said, "Here you go." I looked at his hand, and he was handing me a ticket to the potluck. "Thank you," I said, shocked and excited.

When I walked into the cafeteria, I saw even more food than I saw standing outside the door. It was amazing to be able to walk around and choose from such a variety of foods. What was more amazing to me was that a stranger had given me access to enjoy this. He saw me standing there, fixated on a scrap of meat, and had compassion for me. He changed my situation from being on the outside looking, to sitting down, enjoying the feast with his act of kindness. I don't know how much of a sacrifice it was for him to give me that ticket, but it meant the world to me. I will never forget that experience, and every time I think about it, I relive the joy that I felt all those years ago.

As I made love and kindness my way of life, my associates responded. Customer Service and Operational Efficiency begin to improve dramatically. Soon, sales and profitability were on target. As I demonstrated acts of kindness to the associates, they started to meet expectations. I was still an Assistant Manager, but my raises and bonuses began to increase. My success became contagious; every Associate in the store wanted to be on my operations team. Company leadership was noticing the change in the environment of the store as well as the improved metrics. The ability to turn around a challenging situation with positive energy and high associate morale was a key factor in my promotion.

The Cumberland store was being pulled in a million directions from the store support center and the customers. Leadership needed to raise the standards without killing the Associate's morale. As a Co-Manager, I was equal to the Store Manager on the leadership flowchart. I quickly realized that someone had to take the lead role. The Store Manager had been in the position for almost a year. When I arrived, I asked what he wanted to see the team accomplish and I committed to help make it happen. I told him that I could help him reach his personal career goals and achieve his vision for the store. This defused any perception of competition between us. I was confident that anything God had for me was mine, and I did not have to compete for it. What I could give to the Store Manager was unwavering support and alignment. I made it my focus to consistently provide this.

My attitude of kindness and recognition towards the Associates made a considerable impact. I convinced the Store Manager that we should conduct Associate Appreciation Events. There was no budget for this, so we paid for the first one on our own. After the Store Manager saw the impact that these appreciation meals had on the team, he was on board the kindness train. It was not long before the store was exceeding expectations.

With my promotion came a sizeable salary increase that resolved my monetary concerns. It was a huge relief to put worry about bills behind me. What proved to be most exhilarating was the opportunity to be generous towards others. I got more out of being kind to others than I could imagine. Generosity was kindness on steroids. I would pay for people's order in the drive-thru at Starbucks or Chick fil A. I paid for people's groceries at the grocery store.

I remember one time a lady started crying when I paid for her groceries. She told the cashier to stop ringing up items when the total got to a certain amount. I stepped up and told her to go ahead and get everything she had in her cart. She looked surprised and said, "Really?"

I said, "Yes, I'm sure." When the cashier finished ringing up the items, the lady gave her the money she had. I told the cashier to return her money and that I was going to pay for all of it. The lady burst into tears. She told me she had been out of work for months and had just started a new job. She would not get her first check for another week, so these groceries had to last her until then. She was so thankful. It made my week knowing that she had money and food to last until she got her first paycheck.

One of my favorite ways to show generosity was in restaurants. I would pick a table or two and tell the waitress to bring me their check. I asked the waitress not to tell the customer who was paying for their meal. I was always on the lookout for police, firefighters, or military members to purchase their meals. A few times, the people found out that I had paid for their bill before leaving.

Making the commitment to take on God's nature of generosity is something that anyone can do at any time. Once you receive His love, love and kindness become your foundation. No matter where you are financially, emotionally, or otherwise, adopting a heart of generosity towards others will expand your heart. As your heart for others increases, you will begin to develop in His nature. As we develop in His nature, God will extend the invitation to co-labor with Him. Co-laboring is the pathway to promotion, increased influence, expansion of your assignment and much more. Once we accept His love that is offered through Jesus, we receive a heart transplant. As a result, we are empowered to love with God's love. His love will draw us to generosity as a way of life.

Don't let thoughts of not having enough stall your progress. The little boy with the two fish and five loaves of bread didn't have enough to feed the thousands of people (Luke 9:13-17). He could have thought only of himself and kept his lunch. Instead, he was generous enough to give his entire lunch to Jesus. If you recall, this story ended with everyone eating their fill and twelve baskets of food left over. I'm not telling you to give all of your food away. I am urging you to develop

God's heart for others around you. Then, respond to His promptings without being limited by what you perceive is not enough. Co-laboring with Him in small things builds your trust in Him and lays the foundation for great exploits.

I often think about the example that Jesus made about the widow and her two-mite offering (Mark 12: 41-44). In spite of her poverty, Jesus acknowledged her heart. He said that she gave more than those who were rich and contributed large amounts. Generosity is not measured in quantity only but the quality of the heart matters.

Giving while I was experiencing financial lack taught me to trust God's provision. If I waited until I had enough money to become generous, I would still be broke. If my focus remained on getting myself situated financially, I would still be struggling.

Poverty is a mindset. I know because I lived in poverty. I grew up in poverty and thought I would never escape it. Poverty cannot be legislated away. There may be temporary relief from the symptoms, but the issue will remain. Without a change of heart and mindset, the symptoms recur in time. You can do an internet search on previous lottery winners and verify this. Not all lottery winners return to a financially unstable situation, but many of them do.

Becoming generous where you are elevates you as you help others. I remember reading the question "Are you living your life like a river or a reservoir?" A river provides life giving water everywhere it flows. In contrast, a reservoir holds the water in one place. I wanted to be like a river so I prayed and asked God to show me how and where I could give of my time, talent, and resources. It wasn't long before I started getting ideas that made a huge impact on others.

There was a year when the country was experiencing gas shortages. People had to leave home for work hours early to sit in line at the gas station. Many times, stations would run out of gas with customers in line.. During this time, I thought about how much more difficult things were for my hourly associates. As I began having conversations with them, I found out that some missed days at work because they didn't have enough gas or money for gas. Some even had to choose between gas and food.

Hearing the need for food, I immediately started a food pantry at the store. I went and bought bulk breakfast, lunch, and dinner meals for the store associates. I made sure that everyone knew that when they came to work, they didn't have to worry about eating. I assigned a team to monitor the levels and notify me before we ran out of food. After a while, my team reported that the food wasn't lasting as long as it should. Some of my associates were taking food home. The team suggested to post a sign that forbade taking food home. I didn't mind people taking food to their families and determined to order food more often.

My only concern was that we kept enough food on hand. The food pantry lasted for about two years before people stopped needing help. I didn't ask the company to reimburse my expenses; I was glad to help because I considered it the right thing to do.

The Home Depot provides financial support to employees during difficult times through The Homer Fund. The fund was started by the company's founders, Bernie Marcus, and Arthur Blank. The fund matches donations that the store raises when one of their associates experiences an unforeseen hardship. Over the years, this fund has provided millions of dollars to support for medical bills, funeral expenses, physical rehabilitation, emergency housing, and other emergencies. While the fund will support some situations directly, other times it only matches the donations that the store associates donate as a team. There were times when one of my associates experienced a set-back that qualified for the matching fund but very few people responded with donations. I realized that I needed to model and teach my team about generosity.

I began talking about caring for one another and the different ways that each team member was needed for our store to be successful. I shared how the company provided tools for us to support ourselves and one another. The Homer fund and the 401K program were the examples that I used. These discussions became key elements at our morning and evening meetings, as well as my staff meetings.

Initially, it was disheartening to witness associates not participating in the 401K program. I was relentless in my approach. Soon, almost the entire store would participate in the 401K program and The Homer fund.

I was so excited when my associates would stop me to show their 401K statements. They were grateful that I loved them enough to insist that they invest in their future. They realized that their well-being was a priority for me. Mutual love and sharing created a sense of family. From this foundation of family, we achieved goals that others thought were impossible for the Cascade store. It began with my prayer for God to show me how I could be generous to those around me.

I cannot count the times that I have shown this type of spontaneous generosity. I made it my focus to go out of my way with kindness and generosity every time an opportunity presented itself. I have seen people cry tears of joy in grocery stores, and grown men would tear up after I paid for their tank of gas. It fills my heart with joy as I recall these experiences.

Connecting to the Kingdom

Another area that I became more generous in was tithing and giving to my local church and other organizations that reach the poor. I gave consistently to my church even when I was facing dire financial situations. I made it an automatic response to give back ten percent of what God allowed me to earn. It was a matter of my gratefulness towards God for everything he provided in my life. I learned another level of being generous towards God that transformed my perspective on giving. By connecting my life and career to the Gospel of Jesus Christ, I experienced super abundant increase in my finances.

The easiest way to explain what I mean by connecting my career to the Gospel is to show you an example in the Bible. Luke 4:38-42 gives the account of Jesus entering Peter's house and healing his mother-in-law of a fever. Jesus then began to heal the many people that followed him to Peter's house. Jesus spent the night there and left at daybreak. Everywhere Jesus went He proclaimed that He was fulfilling the call to preach the gospel to the poor, heal the broken hearted, preach deliverance to the captive, the recovery of sight to the blind, to set at liberty those who were bruised, and to preach the acceptable year of the Lord, (see Luke 4:18). There is little reason to doubt that He shared this message with Peter and his household that evening. This is important because this shows that Peter spent time with Jesus hearing His Word.

In Luke 5:1-11, We see Jesus standing by a lake where a great crowd of people had gathered around Him to hear the word of God. You may know the story. Peter and his friends had been fishing all night and had caught nothing. They were washing their nets so that they could go home. Peter and his team were probably exhausted, and a bit discouraged from a hard night's toil with nothing to show for it.

Jesus wanted to teach the crowd of people who had gathered to hear Him. Jesus got in the fishing boat and asked Peter to take him out onto the lake. Peter honored the request and allowed Jesus to teach the crowd the Word of God from his boat. Being out on the water allowed Jesus's voice to be heard by the large crowd of people along the shore.

After Jesus finished teaching the people, He instructed Peter to "Launch out into the deep and let down your nets for a haul." Peter was truly exhausted and reminded Jesus that they had fished all night and had caught nothing. Peter then remembered who he was talking to. This was the man who had healed his mother-in-law of a fever and the many other sick and lame who followed Him to Peter's house. After recalling the miracles, Peter said "Nevertheless, at your Word, I will let down the net. Jesus asked Peter to let down multiple nets, but Peter agreed to let down one net.

What happened next was miraculous. Peter's net caught such a large quantity of fish that it began to break. Peter had to call out to another boat for help. The haul of fish nearly sank both boats. After he brought the huge catch of fish to shore, Peter fell down in front of Jesus and said, "Depart from me, I am a sinful man." I often wondered why he made this statement to Jesus. I believe I now know why. Jesus had clearly instructed Peter to let down his nets, meaning more than one. Peter decided that he wasn't going to bother re-washing the nets that he and his men had just finished cleaning. Instead, Peter used a net that was old and no longer in preferred condition. Despite his disobedience, Jesus still blessed Peter with the catch of his life. Some believe that the catch of fish was so large that it provided over a year's salary for the fishermen. This catch would financially take care of the families of Peter, James, and John while they became fishers of men.

Peter and his partners went from toiling all night with nothing to show for it, to making a year's wages in a single haul. This was made possible by spending enough time with Jesus to trust Him and follow His instructions to partner or connect their business to the gospel. When Peter let Jesus use his boat to teach the people, he was providing a solution to a need in Jesus's ministry. When we spend time with Jesus and allow Him to show us where to connect our careers, businesses, or lives to the gospel, abundant provision becomes available.

I experienced this provision in my life. I developed such a heart for what God wanted to do in the lives of others that I gladly invested my time and resources into the Gospel. I wasn't doing it out of necessity, it was an honor for me to give so that others could hear about God's love. I remember when my mailbox was always full of bills, past due notices, and collection letters. It was depressing to go to the mailbox. Creditors were calling so often that I didn't want to answer my phone. God delivered me from all the stress and anxiety of debt and gave me a new life. I wanted to help as many people experience peace and financial freedom as I could. Connecting my career to extending the Gospel became a source of joy in my life.

Can you imagine the eternal implications of Jesus teaching and healing the multitudes by the shore of the lake that day? Just think about the lives and destinies that were changed because of that encounter with the gospel. Peter's partnership with Jesus helped that impartation happen. There were generational shifts made that day as people experienced the gospel and miracles. They surely went home and told their family, friends, and neighbors. Only in eternity will we be able to find out the size of the harvest of souls and the seeds of destiny that that were planted that day. Peter and his fishing partners now share in the eternal reward for partnering with Jesus.

Once I received the revelation of how God views partnership with the gospel, it changed my focus towards work, career, and money. As an Assistant Manager, I qualified to receive up to twenty five percent of my annual salary in a bonus. The last year that I worked in that role, I wasn't just working to get a check, a promotion, or a bonus. I was working to be able to partner financially with helping spread the Gospel. Every area of operational execution or customer engagement I took added a level of focus for me. I wanted to maximize my bonus because I had committed to give the total bonus as an offering. No one asked me to do this but rather it was in my heart. It was an overflow of love towards people that I didn't know and may never meet, who needed to hear the Gospel. I remember getting the bonus statement in advance of the actual bonus payout. I was so excited to see how much impact my offering was going to make. There were times in my career that I would have viewed this as a loss or something that I gave away. My mindset was now on connecting to God's kingdom and giving into the lives of others, not giving my bonus away. I was excited as I recalled the verse that God loves a cheerful giver.

> "You must each decide in your heart how much to give. And don't give reluctantly or in response to pressure. 'For God loves a person who gives cheerfully.' " — *2 Corinthians 9:7*

It was during this same year that I was promoted from Assistant Manager to Co-Store Manager. This meant that a portion of my bonus was weighted at a higher base salary and a higher percentage, now as a Store Manager. At the time Store Managers could receive a bonus level up to fifty percent of their salary. What started as a commitment to partner with the Gospel and to financially connect my career to the Kingdom had grown to become a year of life changing promotion.

If you have not already done so, I challenge you to spend time seeking God and inquiring where He wants you to connect with the gospel. Finances are not the only way to connect, so a lack of finances is not a way out. There is something that you do or can provide that would be of benefit to the kingdom of God. If you ask, He will show you, He will let you know how you can connect in love. We established earlier that love and trust go hand in hand. If you don't trust God's love, you won't follow through on His instructions. Develop trust by spending time with Him and you will be on your way to becoming a partner with the kingdom of God.

Philanthropy

After I remarried, I convinced my wife that my passion for spontaneous generosity would not be detrimental to our household finances. Like a great partner always does, she helped focus and refine my charity into philanthropy. Together we have done everything from giving people groceries and gas to gifting an all-expense-paid trip to Disney World for a family of four. We have gifted a debt-free car and a couple a debt-free house. I am not bragging on us. I want you to see how kindness and generosity can grow and increase your capacity to bless others.

In 2015, my wife and I founded The Launch Pad Foundation. The non-profit uses property that we purchased and renovated as transitional housing for homeless single parents. Participants move into a fully furnished townhome and receive life skill classes to get them out of homelessness and into sustainable living. The joy of seeing single mothers and their children grow and develop the skills needed to become independent is impressive.

The Bible says," Give, and it shall be given unto you, good measure, pressed down, shaken together, and running over," (Luke 6:38). I am a witness that this is true. The running over experience has been the level of joy I receive from seeing people's lives changed.

From a leadership perspective, kindness helped keep me focused on the conditions of others. Understanding the needs of associates and customers at a personal level became second nature to me. This is a powerful business skill. Being able to anticipate customers' needs gives you the advantage over competitors who react after the fact. This advantage changed my life and career.

God told me to make love and kindness my lifestyle, take my focus off myself, and see how I could help others. I am glad that I listened and obeyed. These are principles that will work for anyone. I encourage you to embrace them if you have not already. Maybe it is an excellent time to revisit your levels of kindness and generosity. Above all, I pray that you will engage in a relationship with the Father, and whatever He tells you to do, do it.

APPENDIX A

HOW DO YOU SEE YOURSELF?

	Slave	Servant	Son
	Slave	**Servant**	**Son**
Your Focus	Self-reliant	Religion	Personal Relationship
	Hands	Head	Heart
	"Doing" all you can do to provide your own solutions without God	"Driven" to succeed and seeking to follow all the rules that should lead to success	"Being" God's Beloved Son because you are embracing His unconditional love
Characterized by	Toil "Lust of the flesh"	Labor "Pride of life"	Rest
Which produces	Anxiety/Fear	Frustration	Peace Co-Laboring
Symbolic Representation	Tower of Babel	O.T. Temple Law & Sacrifices	Your Body is the Temple of the Holy Spirit
Status	Disconnected	Transactional	Relational
Scripture	Ephesians 2:12 NIV	Deuteronomy 28:1	Romans 8:17 NIV

How Do You See Yourself?

APPENDIX B

The Meeting

S pending time with God is vital in the life of a believer. We are instructed throughout the Bible to receive the Word of God as regularly as we consume natural food. Taking time to meditate on the scriptures allows us to digest or process its truth for our specific needs.

Like many, my focus on this important matter varied based on several factors. I intended to do well in this area but failed to make it a consistent part of my life. This changed when my life completely fell apart. I ran to God with my crushed heart and the mess that I had made of my life. Spending time praying, reading, and meditating on the Bible became the most consistent thing in my life. I received strength to endure the darkest season of my life by spending time in God's presence with His Word.

The quiet time I spent with God resulted in the strategies and steps that transformed my life. As things turned around, I became inconsistent in sharing my day with Him. With promotions, marriage, and family to manage, my once relentless pursuit of God and His Word became distracted. God loves us and desires for us to invite Him to share our lives with Him. God won't force His way onto our schedule, but He is always available when we come with open hearts.

While I was struggling with my consistency, God asked me a question. "If you had the opportunity to meet with your favorite billionaire each morning, would you take advantage of it?" I thought for a moment, smiled, and may have even verbalized out loud what I was thinking, "Yes sir, I would." God didn't have to follow with another statement, I guess you could say He dropped the mic at that point. I didn't need any additional encouragement. I made the decision and took the necessary steps to make spending time with God and His Word my lifestyle.

Now it's your turn. If your favorite billionaire or thought leader invited you to have daily meetings, would you take advantage of it? How would you respond if you received that email or phone call, today? These meetings would need to be early since people of this caliber are extremely busy. Would you be willing to adjust your schedule? You might have to go to bed early to be alert during the meetings. Some of your favorite television shows might have to be recorded or missed so that you could prepare. Would you do it?

During the meetings, would you do all the talking, or would you allow the person you are meeting with to share? Most of us would jump at the chance to have a single meeting of this magnitude. We would pay a handsome price and be flexible to any schedule requirements. Commitment to follow the advice given during this session would be unparalleled. Yet, we have that open invitation, even more.

Every day, God is extending the invitation for you to spend time with Him and listen to what He has to say. The Creator of Heaven and Earth, the Founder of Wisdom and Understanding calls out to us daily.

APPENDIX C

THE CALL TO SONSHIP

S ince Jesus's resurrection from the dead, the invitation to join the family of God has been available. Throughout the age of the Church the picture of our place in God's family has become clearer and clearer. Now more than ever there is a need to understand that believers are being called, beckoned even commanded to take our place as sons and daughters. God is waiting for us as His sons and daughters to awaken to our identity and take our proper places. The Father's call is for us to be matured in His nature and aligned with His assignment for our lives. These assignments cover every sector of society. The whole creation echoes the Father's call as a cry for the revealing of the sons of God. Romans 8:19 confirms this. *For the eagerly awaiting creation waits for the revealing of the sons of God.* All of creation cries out for the revealing of those who have been transformed by love, who co-labor with the Father to bring solutions, elevation, cures, inventions, and rest. The call goes out from the fields of education, business, government, family, arts and entertainment, media, and the church.

The need for sonship has been established. God has provided access to our change of status. Galatians 4:6 reminds us of this. *And because you are sons, God sent the spirit of His son into our hearts crying Abba Father.* It is up to us to embrace the status that has been made available. The revealing or unveiling of Sonship happens within us. We must believe that we are called into Sonship. In Luke Jesus told the story of the

Prodigal Son. The younger of two sons asked his father for his part of the inheritance in advance. After receiving his inheritance, he went away and foolishly squandered it all away. Being destitute accepted a job feeding pigs. His situation was so dire that he wanted the pig's food for himself. The Bible says that he then *came to himself.* He remembered that he was a son and that His father had servants who always had food to spare. His situation caused him to forget who he was because of his behavior and predicament. Selfish ambition and pride consumed him and led him to demand his inheritance. Shame and regret for his actions covered his mind after he lost everything he had. But one day he came to himself and remembered that he was a son. He returned to his father hoping to become a servant but was received as a son.

Past mistakes and failures do not nullify sonship. When I wasted my stock portfolio and had nothing to show for it, the guilt and shame was heavy. God did not judge me by my mistakes, He only considered that Jesus had paid a dear price to bring me back to Him. Once I came to myself and reached out to Him, He accepted me. He did not regulate me to second class status, but as a fully vested son. I had to work through my bad beliefs that tied me to servant status, but God accepted me as a Son. When I realized that He did not want me as His servant, I had to renew my mind to all that Sonship status changed (see Romans 12:1-2).

We cannot co-labor with Him if we hold on to a servant's mindset. We must become sons who wholeheartedly serve in love. The servant mindset will keep us confined to the extent of our performance and failures. This containment of our focus reduces the area of our impact to inside the four walls of the church and a few select areas beyond them. This is largely due to fear to operate in the marketplace. Relying on our own abilities and performance opens us to this fear. We have been delivered from fear. *There is no fear in love, but perfect love casts out fear: because fear has to do with punishment. The one who fears is not made perfect in love (1 John 4:18-19 NIV).*

Embracing love delivers us from fear. Every time fear shows up it should be a reminder that we have been delivered from it. We must refuse to fear and remain focused on God's love for us. Fear comes to make us focus on ourselves. When we place our focus on our own promotion, safety, or wellbeing, we are taking our eyes off God's love for us. Placing ourselves in the center of attention gives fear access into our lives. It serves us well to keep Romans 8:15 in our hearts. *For you have not received a spirit of slavery that returns you to fear, but you received the Spirit of sonship by whom we cry Abba! Father.* The word Abba translated means Daddy. When one of my children needs me, they call me Daddy not Father. While I am their father, the title sounds formal and distant compared to Daddy. God wants us in intimate relationship with Him to the extent that we call Him Daddy when we need Him.

Co-laboring with God will produce transformation in your business, marriage, ministry, and career. Entire sectors of society will be impacted as sons and daughters respond to the call and show up. Jesus only did what he saw His Father doing. This shows the level of relationship they shared. We must become dependent on Him for our directions, strategy, and responses. The validation of sonship is not in exploits, but rather in being led by God. *For as many as are led by the spirit of God, these are the sons of God (Romans 8:14).* Our focus is on being led and He provides the transformations, exploits and miracles.

All of creation is crying out for the revealing of those who have been transformed by love, who co-labor with the father to bring solutions, elevation, cures, inventions, and rest. The call goes out from the fields of education, business, government, family, arts and entertainment, media, and the Church. Have you come to yourself; will you answer the call?

READ MORE!

There are **more valuable resources like *ELEVATED*** available to help continue your journey of how-to co-labor with God.

Visit www.parablesmedia.com and take your next steps to joining countless others whose lives are being transformed and co-laboring with God to transform their spheres of influence with the impact of the Kingdom of God.

Parables Media

Have Questions?

Send your questions or thoughts to: info@parablesmedia.com

AUTHOR BIO

K enneth Hill (Kenny) is a father, non-profit executive, minister, speaker, author, real estate developer and coach. Kenneth is a natural leader who has always had a passion for helping people. At an early age, he learned the importance of serving others and giving back. This outlook has produced success at home, in business, and in the community.

Kenneth was raised by a single mother and is the eldest of seven children. As a child, he worked hard to help his mom and support the family. He worked at The Home Depot to pay his way through college and received his Bachelor of Arts in Economics from the University of California, San Diego. After 30 years of service, Kenneth retired from

The Home Depot and founded The Launch Pad Foundation. This non-profit provides housing, life skills, and career training to homeless single mothers. The Launch Pad Foundation sponsors monthly community clean ups along the Martin Luther King Jr Blvd in Atlanta, GA as well as literacy support programs for elementary school aged children.

Kenneth answered the call to ministry in 2000 and excels in the application of biblical principles and spiritual laws in the marketplace. His faith in God, community activism, and desire to serve others have played large roles in his life. Kenneth embraces leadership opportunities and advocates for those whose voices are not heard. Kenneth is a member of the Christian Business Men's Connection (CBMC), a board member of the 100 Black Men of America, South Metro Atlanta Chapter, and a life member of Kappa Alpha Psi Fraternity. He is married to Clarisa, and they have two daughters. Kenneth is living his dream and is striving to help others achieve theirs.

LOVE THIS BOOK?
DON'T FORGET TO LEAVE A REVIEW!

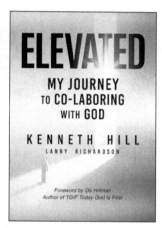

Every review matters and it matters a *lot!*
Head over to Amazon or wherever you purchased this book.
to leave an honest review for me.
I thank you endlessly.

Next Steps to Your Elevation

"Humble yourselves before the LORD, and He will exalt you." — *James 4:10 (ESV)*

- **Access additional Parables Media Resources** as you seek to co-labor with God here –www.parabelsmedia.com/resources
- **Begin taking steps of faith** as you apply the principles outlined in the book by purchasing – ELEVATED – The Workbook
- **Contact the Parables Media Follow Up Team** with your questions here – info@parablesmedia.com

"… It is written, 'Man shall not live by bread alone, but by every word that comes from the mouth of God.' " — *Matthew 4:4 (ESV)*

www.parablesmedia.com

CPSIA information can be obtained
at www.ICGtesting.com
Printed in the USA
JSHW010915060322
23434JS00002B/2

9 781662 835346